Grit & Gratitude

Real Life. Real Problems. Real Success – With God.

JEN GUIDRY

Brilliantly Bold Books

Published by Brilliantly Bold Books

ISBN: 979-8-9888315-2-5 (Hardback)
ISBN: 979-8-9888315-0-1 (Paperback)
ISBN: 979-8-9888315-1-8 (eBook)

Unless otherwise noted, Scripture quotations marked (NIV) are taken from the New International Version, copyright ©1973, 1978, 1984, 2011 by Biblica, Inc. Used by permission of Zondervan. All rights reserved worldwide.

Scripture quotations marked (NKJV) are taken from the New King James Version. Copyright ©1982 by Thomas Nelson, Inc. Used by Permission. All rights reserved.

Book Cover Design by Suzanne Pack
Interior design: Bryana Anderle (YouPublish.com)
Interior art direction: Chad Harrington (YouPublish.com)

Printed in the United States of America

This is a must-read book! *Grit and Gratitude* had me at page one. It is a moving and honest account of overcoming tribulation and trauma through faith and a positive mindset. The chapter "Praying in an Uber" was so real and authentic which really struck close to home for me.

This book explains in detail the walk with God and how it can make an impact on handling the obstacles that life throws at us. The author's positive and "can-do" perspective is amazing, and I thoroughly recommend this book as a reminder to all of us that adversity does not have to define us. By changing your perspective, you can change the world!

— Dr. Robb Kelly PhD

Jen Guidry's book, Grit and Gratitude could not be titled more perfectly. The book reads as smooth as a milk chocolate and as raw as a child's tears. It's as if you are sharing a cup of tea with an old friend, trusting in their confidence. None of us get through life without a bump in the road and this book is an inspiration, as well as an affirmation, that God's love always prevails. Grit and Gratitude is the perfect gift for yourself or someone you love.

— Diane Gottsman
National Etiquette Expert, Author
The Protocol School of Texas

Grit and gratitude is a perfect way to describe this new book carefully written by Jen Guidry! Her strength of character and gratitude for her blessings leads me to read this book with hope and learn how to make my life better. Thank you!

— Dian G.

Grit and Gratitude felt like a conversation with a close friend reminding me to stop and take time to appreciate the things I often take for granted.

Life gets busy for all of us, and we can get stuck focusing on the wrong things. This book reminds us to show gratitude to God for all the wonderful people and moments we have in our lives.

— Lori P.

Jen has walked the walk and so, when she talks, she does it with a strong and true voice that resonates and relates to the human experience. It is like listening to a wise and trusted friend. A true gift to those who are lucky enough to find her book.

— Debbie M.

Dedication

As my book takes flight into the world, it is bound by threads of love, guided by the hands of God, and adorned with immeasurable gratitude. I find myself swimming in a sea of emotions, and the deep currents of our love rush through my heart, carrying me forward as I pen this heartfelt dedication.

Michael, you are not just my partner in life, but the very essence of love that tenderly breathes life into my soul. Your unwavering support and encouragement have been the bedrock upon which my dreams have flourished. With every word I weave onto these pages, I am continually reminded of the beautiful tapestry we have woven together, one stitched together by boundless love and tireless devotion.

Our love story is like a beautifully written chapter, where every word echoes with the melody of joy, and each turn of a page reveals a deeper connection that words alone cannot capture. It is a story woven with golden strands of laughter, wrapped in the warmth of understanding, and embellished with the courage to weather life's storms hand in hand.

There are not enough words in any language to express the depth of my love for you, Michael. My heart overflows with love, gratitude, and awe, knowing that our love story will forever be synonymous with the words "forever" and "always."

Your loving wife,

Jen

.

Contents

Introduction

I want this book to be like having a conversation with your best friend, as though we are sitting around your kitchen table with a cup of coffee in hand, talking about the things that every woman has felt, gone through, or wanted to say. I am listening.

I will share things with you about my past—things I have gone through and lessons I have learned along the way—and my hope is that you will see how a life with God is so much better than a life without. I believe it is our duty to share our stories with others so that we can know we are not alone in our struggles and our thoughts.

My hope is that my stories will inspire you to see things a little differently than you do now, that your mind may be opened to new possibilities, and that you will take comfort in knowing that if I can overcome with God by my side, you can too.

Some of this book was written before I married Michael. So you will see references to me being both single and married. When I refer to my hubs, I am talking about my darling, Michael, whom I married October 10, 2020.

So sit back and relax. Let's enjoy this fellowship together.

Part 1

Choices

*"Every time you make a choice you are turning the
central part of you, the part of you that chooses,
into something a little different from what it was
before. And taking your life as a whole, with all
your innumerable choices, all your life long you
are slowly turning this central thing either into a
heavenly creature or into a hellish creature . . ."*

– *Mere Christianity* by C. S. Lewis

I know, I just went really deep right from the get-go. We need to talk about this though, because it is of utmost importance. We have the choice to do just about anything in our lives. We are presented with choices every day. Every single choice you have made has made you . . . you.

Chapter 1

Duty vs. Love

I have found myself saying the words, "I *have* to _____" a lot lately and the mindset that comes with that attitude makes me resentful of whatever it is. We do that often, don't we?

I have felt as though I was stuck doing things I didn't want to do, stupid stuff like going to work, cooking dinner, doing the laundry . . . you get the point. It is funny how a negative attitude is like a snowball rolling down a hill. Once you start going down that path, it is easy to find other things that you *have to* do and then hate every one of them along the way.

On a Monday morning, I was talking to my mom, telling her I *had* to go to work. Once I said it, the realization came to me that I *get* to go to work. It is a privilege to help people every day. Thank you, Jesus. I needed to change the way I saw things . . . quickly. I was not doing what God has called us to do. I was whining, not putting love into whatever came before me.

God calls us to be imitators of Christ. To spread His word throughout the nations. To Declare His glory. To not grow weary of doing good. To love one another.

Yet we get so focused on the destination, that many of us forget the journey along the way. We know that we are supposed to do all of these things and we work diligently toward them, but we forget to inject them into *everything* we do, including work. What better way is there to inject love

(God's love) into your day and the day of everyone around you than to perform your tasks, obligations, and chores with love in your heart?

Hear me out as I talk about duty versus love.

Duty is packing your spouse a lunch. Love is putting a nice note inside.

Duty is making your spouse coffee in the morning. Love is bringing coffee to them with a dance and a smile.

Duty is hopping out of bed the second the alarm goes off. Love is making time for five minutes of morning snuggles.

Duty is finishing your assigned task early and blowing off the rest of your workday. Love is asking if anyone else needs help.

Duty is saying, "That's not *my* job, sorry." Love is rolling up your sleeves to assist.

Duty is saying goodbye to your loved one with a quick obligatory peck on the cheek. Love is stopping what you are doing to get up and give your sweetie a long, purposeful hug.

When you do things with love in your heart, the task is no longer a burden.

The chore becomes a cakewalk.

The imposition becomes a blessing.

The requirement becomes a pleasure.

The next time you find yourself just doing your job or going through the motions, stop yourself. This is a perfect time to show God's love to someone else. Perform whatever it is with love . . . and then watch the smile that appears on your face and the face of others. Know that God is smiling too.

------------------------------------◆------------------------------------

If I speak in the tongues of men or of angels, but do not have love, I am only a resounding gong or a clanging cymbal. If I have the gift of prophecy and can fathom all mysteries and all knowledge, and if I have a faith that can move mountains, but do not have love, I am nothing. If I give all I possess to the poor and give over my body to hardship that I may boast, but do not have love, I gain nothing. 1 Corinthians 13:1–3

Dear friends, let us love one another, for love comes from God. Everyone who loves has been born of God and knows God. 1 John 4:7

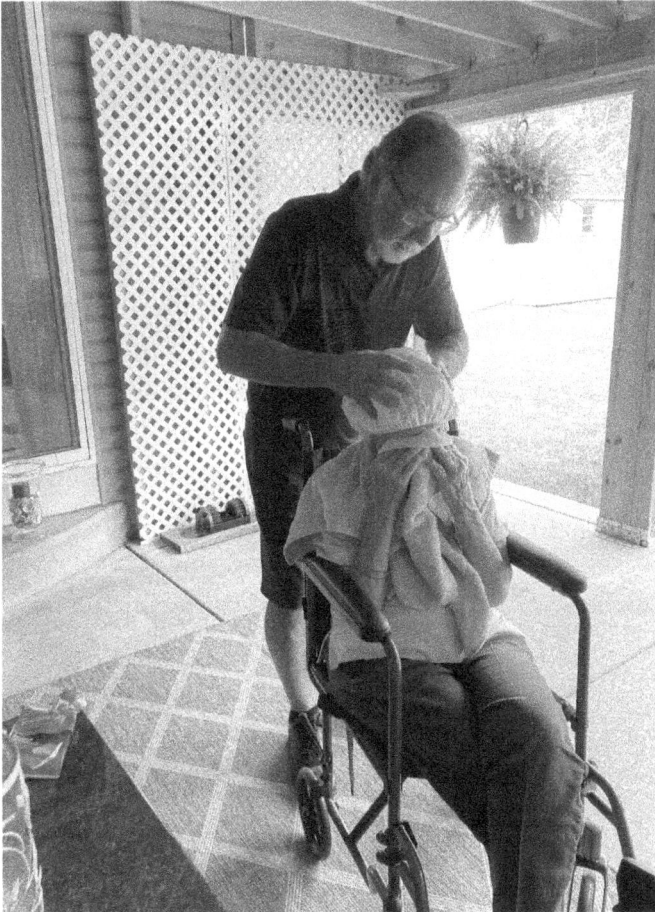

An act of love. Dad washing grandma's hair.

Chapter 2

I Think

When I was younger, I believed I wasn't worthy of love. Not real love anyway. I didn't know what that was and honestly, I thought it was not possible. Fairytales and butterflies, *That is not how life works,* I thought.

So my decisions and the actions that came from that belief led me to make a lot of relationship mistakes when it came to my love life. Boy, did I settle for the wrong men. I didn't think that I deserved better, so I made one poor choice after another.

As my relationship with God has grown, I have realized that what we tell ourselves is so important. Our thoughts direct the paths our lives take. One tiny thought, one certain way of looking at things, one feeling, judgment, and reaction at a time, day after day. They all add up to get you to who you are as a person today.

They have shaped your physical health, a great deal of your mental health, your personality, and your spirituality most likely without you realizing it. Day by day, thought by thought, here you are. What kind of person are ya?

Don't like where you are? Change your way of thinking. It is that simple. Make different choices. Train yourself to have better thoughts. The transformation will follow. That is what I did and have continued to do all throughout my journey with God. You can too.

Throughout the Bible, God encourages us to raise the bar on our standards of everyday life by thinking and responding differently, in a new way. An amazing thing happens when we do such a thing . . . we rise up to meet it. Raise the bar and rise up to meet it.

Do not conform to the pattern of this world, but be transformed by the renewing of your mind. Then you will be able to test and approve what God's will is—his good, pleasing and perfect will. Romans 12:2

Chapter 3

Choices and Things

I know, I talk a lot about choices. It is an important topic to think about!

We all have choices. Every day. Every moment. Choices about how we want to start our day. When we wake up. Who we spend time with. You have bazillions of choices. This book would be too long if I listed them all.

The current version of me (and you) is a culmination of my (or your) choices.

Sometimes, I just sit and think about where I am today. I am here, on my comfy couch with my dog, Bella, curled up next to me. I remember the day I got her eleven years ago. The second I saw her, I loved her. I have a smile on my face now, and I am grateful for the moments I get to share with my faithful companion.

I remember a time when I lived a very different life . . . when I was too busy to appreciate anything, and my decisions were made solely based upon what *I* wanted to do. If anyone got in my way, I ran them over (not literally, don't worry!). I didn't have God in my life and, trust me, you could tell. I was going to live *my* way and do as I pleased. While some things worked out well, the stuff that mattered, did not.

The Jen that was back then is not the same Jen that exists today. I will tell you though, the journey is not an easy one. I believe I will continue to be in this undertaking for the rest of my life. It is all about choices and action.

Some think that once they accept Jesus into their hearts everything in life is going to be smooth sailing. That is not true. Though your heart changes and you are transformed into a new being, you still have to act.

God has our lives planned. Yes, *all* of us. He sees what *can* be if we take Him along the ride with us. He knows every hair on our heads and every heartache we go through. We have a choice—to acknowledge Him or not, to ignore Him or invite Him into our lives, to make choices that He beckons us to make or to do things that are against His will. Shocker alert—the whole going against His will thing never ends well. I am sure you probably have figured this out already.

There are a lot of people who have a false belief that God will take care of us and magically make everything in our life better or easy, like we don't have to put in any effort. We use that as an excuse to not do anything and then have the audacity to blame God when things don't work out the way we think they should have.

We don't want to do the hard thing or go through difficult times because we don't think that we should have to.

We think, "If God wanted me to do this, then he would just do it. I shouldn't have to work for it."

Hogwash.

Remember the old parable about the guy standing on his roof in a flood? A man with a rowboat comes. "No thanks, God will save me."

Then the speedboat. "No thanks, waiting for God."

Then the helicopter. "Nope!"

Then the guy dies, and God is like, "Dude! I sent three people to save you, what else did you expect?"

The point is this: Our choices, while we have them, we also have to insert action into them. You can't decide to lose weight and then do nothing to help lose weight.

God will help us, but we also have to help ourselves. It is not a simple as trusting that God will help you through. He does do that . . . but there has to be some action of our own as well.

We cry out, "Save me, Lord!" but we also have to work on saving ourselves.

You can do all things through Christ . . . but you have to actually do something! You can't just sit there idly.

God will be right by our side through every choice we make. We either take him with us, or not . . . it is our choice.

One way is a heck of a lot better though. Bring God with you through *all* of your choices and see what happens.

What good is it, my brothers and sisters, if someone claims to have faith but has no deeds? Can such faith save them? Suppose a brother or a sister is without clothes and daily food. If one of you says to them, "Go in peace; keep warm and well fed," but does nothing about their physical needs, what good is it? In the same way, faith by itself, if it is not accompanied by action, is dead. James 2:14–17

You see that a person is considered righteous by what they do and not by faith alone. James 2:24

Chapter 4

Just Keep Me Company

Getting old. It is inevitable. This is the story of my beautiful grandmother and the choices that most every family has to make at some point. Tough choices. Aging parents. Love. Understanding. Patience. Acceptance. Sacrifice.

It was the last day living in her house and she didn't know it. It was the last coffee made on her own, just like she'd been doing for so many years. Her routine of eggs and toast, reading the newspaper, and watching TV, after so many years, came to an end that day.

I wonder if she would have done anything different, had she known. Probably not. Perhaps she would have savored those sweet moments a little longer—her last lingering moments of living on her own in her home, surrounded by the familiarity of her possessions.

Dementia had reared its ugly head and affected her brain. Sometimes she was completely lucid and other times, not so much. She had her good days and bad ones too. She would forget things she'd just heard but remember details of days long gone. That is the way it works. She acknowledged the fact that her mind just wasn't what it once was and acknowledged that there was nothing she could do about it. The realization had to be a difficult one. I cannot imagine it for myself. It made me love her more if that was possible.

Everything took her longer now. She slept a lot. Ached a lot. Walking was difficult, but she pushed herself to do it anyway. Then the fall happened.

She didn't mean to fall. I mean, who does, anyway? She laid there for quite some time, unable to get herself back up. She cried for help, but no one could hear her—part of the problem of living alone.

Finally, she was able to call her son (my father) and as he rushed over there, he called an ambulance for her. They had to crawl through a window to get to her and by the time he got there, they were ready to transport her to the hospital.

He had been dreading the moment to come. In the back of his mind, he could foresee it. Then it happened. He knew it was only a matter of time, starting with one incident and from that moment on, nothing would ever be the same.

His mother's health had been declining daily, but she was still able to manage on her own. Until one day she could not. That's how it works.

When she woke up in the hospital, she thought that she would get better and go back home to her own comfort. She said many times, "If I can't live in my own house, I don't want to live." The days passed, and she didn't get much better. Instead, she got worse.

They moved her to a rehab facility—to make her better. Days turned into a month, and she could not yet walk. She needed two aides to help her, but she could feed herself. Oh, how she loved to eat!! We always joked that Felicia could eat more than anyone any of us know. For as small and delicate as her frame had become, she could still pack food into that stomach of hers. That brought her some joy.

Her life now consisted of lying in bed, though it wasn't her bed, or sitting up in a chair, and it was not her chair.

Her children talked regularly with each other while trying to figure out the best plan of action for her. What would be best? Did anyone have the ability to take her into their home? So many hard decisions needed to be made. Everyone agreed, though that she could not go back to her own home.

Her security. Her independence. Her peace. Her own bed and coffee and eggs. Her couch and her comfy spots. The front porch that she sat on and watched the world go by. All of those things would never be seen or experienced by her again and that, my friends, was heartbreaking.

If she would have only known.

Then the talk came.

"Mom, you won't be able to go back home again. I am sorry."

Hearing those words was unbearable for her, I am sure. She would have to accept that for the rest of her life, her world was going to be much different than she had hoped.

Blankly, she stared at her son and tried to comprehend the words so gently spoken to her. Did she understand?

"Just keep me company," she said.

She was scared.

His heart broke that day and so did mine. It was a powerful lesson in vulnerability, aging, and acknowledging the unknown, which is uncharted territory for most people. The reality of her situation smacked the family right in the face . . . hard. It won't ever be the same. That is hard to deal with, but we must.

Days we all knew would most likely come, but we still wished they would never arrive. I'm sure you know what I am talking about.

She had already lost her husband of 50+ years and outlived all of her friends and her siblings. In the final stages of her life, she didn't want to be alone. I don't blame her.

So we will do just that, Gram. We'll keep you company.

Do not cast me away when I am old;
do not forsake me when my strength is gone. Psalm 71:9

Stand up in the presence of the aged, show respect for the elderly and revere your God. I am the LORD. Leviticus 19:32

Even to your old age and gray hairs
I am he; I am he who will sustain you.
I have made you and I will carry you;
I will sustain you and I will rescue you. Isaiah 46:4

Chapter 5

One Day, I Will Miss the Water Spots on the Mirror and Your Horrible Morning Breath in My Face

Anyone who is married can understand that there will come a point in time when the little idiosyncrasies that you spouse has . . . well, will annoy you a bit. It is okay to admit it.

Yesterday, after picking up the towel Mike forgot on the floor and after I had cleaned the bathroom mirror speckled with water spots for the second time, I found myself a little put off.

In the midst of grumbling to myself, God smacked me on the side of the head. I had the overwhelming thought that I would surely miss all of these things if he weren't around. I would miss the occasional towel on the floor, the water spots on the mirror, and the horrible morning breath. I would long for them, actually. Crave them. I surely would. I am lucky—*so* lucky—to have a man that loves me like he does.

Such things mean that my love is with me, healthy, and alive.

I will bet you there are millions of widows and widowers who would give *anything* to be able to wake up to the things that once annoyed them about the one they loved.

Suddenly, my tasks were no longer a burden. I smiled and wiped down the mirror again. Then I ran to my husband and gave him a hug.

That is my lesson of the day!

Love is patient, love is kind. It does not envy, it does not boast, it is not proud. It does not dishonor others, it is not self-seeking, it is not easily angered, it keeps no record of wrongs. Love does not delight in evil but rejoices with the truth. It always protects, always trusts, always hopes, always perseveres. Love never fails. 1 Corinthians 13:4–8

My incredible husband and I on our wedding day.

Chapter 6

Doubt and Trust

In our house, we have two sculptures that we picked up in Jerome, AZ made by a Christian artist. The moment I saw them, I loved what they represent.

The first is a man sitting on a huge rock. He is blindfolded and holding a large rock in his hand. His face looks defeated, scared and unsure. He is Doubt.

The other is of a woman standing on a huge rock of her own. She is on the edge of it with one foot up as if she is about to walk off of it. She is also blindfolded, standing with her arms wide open about to take that step, and the expression on her face is that of assurance.

Despite the fact that she is about to walk into the unknown, she gives me the impression that she believes she will be okay. She is Trust.

I am sitting here looking at them, and it makes me think about how these sculptures are such a great depiction of what life is like with and without God.

Doubt makes you question everything and focus on nothing. Nothing has meaning when all you have is doubt. What's the point? Doubt paralyzes you and it stops you from living the life you were meant to live.

Doubt robs you of joy, hope, and confidence and it introduces fear, worry, and uncertainty. Doubt makes us pessimistic about what is to come. Doubt is a real dismal thing.

Trust on the other hand is incredible and extraordinary. It lets you walk with your head held high because you know that God is with you. It brings the realization that He will lead you and He will be with you always. Sure, taking that step off into uncertainty is scary, but you do it anyway because you know Him. Resilience, balance, and sustenance pour into your soul when you trust.

You know that no matter how much you may not understand whatever may be in front of you, God will lead you on the right path. He has great plans for your life, plans for prosperity and a bright future—one we could not imagine for ourselves.

Trust is knowing that God will comfort us and sustain us. God will give us peace—perfect peace—confidence, joy, and protection . . . when you *trust* Him to do so.

Which statue resonates with you more? Which life do you want to live?

Jesus replied, "Truly I tell you, if you have faith and do not doubt, not only can you do what was done to the fig tree, but also you can say to this mountain, 'Go, throw yourself into the sea,' and it will be done.
Matthew 21:21

Trust in the LORD with all your heart
and lean not on your own understanding;
in all your ways submit to him,
and he will make your paths straight. Proverbs 3:5–6

My Sedona statues – doubt and trust.

Chapter 7

Settling for Crumbs

This past weekend, I heated up some chicken and decided to feed it to the dogs for dinner. I knew they could sense my intentions, as all three of them sat down and stared at me like little angels. Three dogs in a row.

I cut the chicken up into a bunch of pieces and starting to feed them. I took turns, feeding them one by one. They scarfed it down and then patiently waited for their turn once again.

Occasionally, a tiny piece would drop to the floor and one dog would stop and frantically search for that tiny piece that fell on the floor, so much so that she would miss her turn. She kept doing it over and over again while the other two weren't phased. They didn't care one bit about the tiny crumbs falling because they knew something better was coming and they were willing to wait for it. They didn't budge and sat there wagging their tails while looking up at me, waiting for the good stuff.

Without realizing it, I kept saying "Sadie, don't worry about those pieces, I have something better for you!" Over and over again. She didn't listen, but that's probably because she doesn't understand English. But I digress. . . .

I bet though, that God wants to shout to us the same phrase, "I have something so much better for you!! You just have to wait. Give up what you have now and don't settle for those crumbs."

It dawned on me: This is what people do. They settle for the crumbs, the mediocrity.

We settle for what is good enough instead for what is great because we don't want to wait and put forth the effort for it.

We need to remember that the crumbs are easy, but when you are constantly going after crumbs, you never get the really good stuff. You can choose to live in either world. It is up to you.

God gives us the good stuff while the devil gives us crumbs.

Finally, brothers and sisters, whatever is true, whatever is noble, whatever is right, whatever is pure, whatever is lovely, whatever is admirable—if anything is excellent or praiseworthy—think about such things. Philippians 4:8

Why spend money on what is not bread,
and your labor on what does not satisfy?
Listen, listen to me, and eat what is good,
and you will delight in the richest of fare. Isaiah 55:2

Chapter 8

Choppin' Tomatoes

Afew days ago, I came home from work much later than I wanted because of a myriad of time blockers. I had to catch up after being in meetings all day and then on my way home I ran into traffic, accidents, etc. A normal, 20-minute drive turned into a 45-minute commute after an already very long and tiring day. I have to admit, I was tired and maybe a little disgruntled. Okay, a lot.

When I got home, my hubs was nowhere to be found. I called him and found out he was still working but would be home soon. He was out the door at six that morning, and it was now a little past seven. Long day. Much longer than mine.

I started making dinner. Now, mind you, I was still a little perturbed, now because I was stuck making dinner and didn't feel like it.

I found myself aggressively chopping tomatoes. In my mind, I actually got angry with Michael for not being there to help me.

Then I had one of my God-smacking-Jennifer-on-the-side-of-the-head moments.

Jennifer!! How blessed are you?

You have a husband that has an outstanding work ethic who loves you unconditionally.

You have food to cook.

I brought you home safely today.

I saw you with your clients and you were great.

I inspired you to help someone today and pray for them.

Look at this home that you have, your family, and those precious dogs!

You are so blessed. These are the things that you need to focus on.

I noticed my tomato chopping became a little less assaultive. I got it. I felt like a bit of a ding dong for being so ungrateful and selfish.

A smile formed on my scowling face. My attitude went from displeasure to enjoyment of my task at hand. I get to cook for my hardworking husband.

Thanks God!

Michael came home a few moments later. Tired and sweaty from a long day of work. I gave him a big hug and a kiss. I was happy he was home.

Sometimes we need these little reminders. I needed it that day. We all do. I think back to how that night could have gone if he came home to a crabby and annoyed Jen. That would not have been good. It would have been selfish of me. I'm glad I keep my heart open to hearing God when He speaks.

He's a lot smarter than me :)

Let the peace of Christ rule in your hearts, since as members of one body you were called to peace. And be thankful. Colossians 3:15

Give thanks in all circumstances; for this is God's will for you in Christ Jesus. 1 Thessalonians 5:18

Chapter 9

Praying in an Uber

God has an interesting way of putting everything in perspective sometimes. Yesterday's "God Moment" was during my Uber ride.

My teammates and I went to a gala yesterday evening, and I decided to Uber there. I got into the car as I have done many other times and tried to make small talk, but I noticed that my driver hardly spoke English. I embarrassingly texted my staff: My driver doesn't speak English. What a judging jerk I was. Even now, I feel so convicted. I am sorry for assuming who she was.

Moments after my mean comment, everything changed.

Something inside me started to take notice of everything in her vehicle.

She had a handicap placard hanging on the rearview mirror. She had a crucifix sitting on the dashboard. She had what appeared to be a rosary wrapped around her left hand.

So I decided to ask her about it. Indeed, it was a rosary wrapped around her hand.

That is when she came alive. . . .

The woman excitedly showed me the rosary and then another one made from rosewood and told me all about them. She also had anointing oil and Holy Water. She was all set!

She told me how she has used her driving as a way to pray for those she meets. She prays for everyone who enters her vehicle.

The smile on her face lit up the entire vehicle, and oddly enough, I understood her.

She talked about how she knows God is with her always and that she cannot wait to meet Him, that she is thankful for her life and the others she gets to meet. She shared with me how seven months prior, she'd undergone a double mastectomy. Then three months after that, she was diagnosed with cancer again, this time in her spine and stage four.

And she was fine with it, because soon she would get to meet her Lord and Savior. She said that she was driving to earn a little extra money while she could and that she used it as a ministry to show others the power of God. Gabriella is a very blessed and amazing woman and I could see the light of God pouring through her. Her beautiful soul was lit up.

The encounter was not what I was expecting when I got into that car, yet it was profoundly more amazing than anything I could have ever thought would happen in an Uber on the way to a gala that I didn't particularly want to go to.

Imagine yourself and what you would do if you were in her situation. Most of us would likely not be using our last days on earth to minister to people. She was, and that's pretty amazing, isn't it? She was listening to God, serving and saving along the way.

When our ride was over, I stayed in the car for a few minutes talking to her. I asked her if I could pray for her right then and there.

I laid my hand on her right shoulder and closed my eyes and bowed my head. I felt the pain she kept inside of her, and I prayed aloud for her with everything that entered my mind.

We cried, and I got out of the car.

Powerful.

Gabriella, I thank you for the beautiful ride, but most of all, for reminding me of the overwhelming love God has for all of us. Keep shining.

"His master replied, 'Well done, good and faithful servant! You have been faithful with a few things; I will put you in charge of many things. Come and share your master's happiness!' Matthew 25:21

You, then, why do you judge your brother or sister? Or why do you treat them with contempt? For we will all stand before God's judgment seat. It is written:

"'As surely as I live,' says the Lord,
'every knee will bow before me;
every tongue will acknowledge God.'"

So then, each of us will give an account of ourselves to God. Romans 14:10–12

They are from the world and therefore speak from the viewpoint of the world, and the world listens to them. We are from God, and whoever knows God listens to us; but whoever is not from God does not listen to us. This is how we recognize the Spirit[a] of truth and the spirit of falsehood. 1 John 4:5–6

Chapter 10

It is *not,* Me, Me, Me!

My friend list has evolved over the years. When I was in my teens and early twenties (I call those years, BG—Before God. Well, before I acknowledged Him, anyway.), my friends were not a good influence on me. I think of that period of my life as the years that I hid from God. Now, I know now that He didn't go anywhere during that time, but I pretended He could not see the things that I was doing. At least then I didn't have to feel guilty about anything.

I was selfish, and I wanted to do things that weren't necessarily in my best interest, and my friends didn't try to stop me. In fact, they encouraged my bad behavior, maybe as an excuse to do the same things themselves. I was a horrible friend.

Fast forward twenty-plus years, my friends and the people who I have aligned myself with are quite different. They would call me out on my nonsense if I had an idea to do something stupid. I also have a lot less friends now.

What I have learned is how the quality of our life is determined in a large part by the quality of our relationships. Who you hang out with is who you become. What does your relationship assortment say about you?

My circle of friends is in no way perfect, but we all subscribe to the same ideology when it comes to our relationships in life: He, we, me. Three little words with profound meaning when put into the right context.

First, there is He: God needs to be the primary relationship in your life. His Word means more than any other word and what His will is for your life should have more potency than any other influence around you. He commands us to, *"Love the Lord your God with all your heart and with all your soul and with all your mind* (Matt. 22:37)." That is the greatest commandment.

When you put God first, you begin to want to emulate His qualities. His good influence rubs off on you. Love, grace, patience, kindness, protection, trust, hope . . . you get the idea. You will be a better person in every way because you have the greatest mentor that ever existed.

When you understand and acknowledge that everything comes from God, you will get it! Take God on as your partner in everything you do, and you will flourish.

Then, We: Selfishness, self-centeredness, and pridefulness dissipate when you have the acute understanding that it isn't all about you. It is not me, it is we. Your family should come second in your relationship mix. Be forgiving. Spend time. Encourage. Love. Put energy into these very special relationships. Give and receive wisdom from these important people in your life.

Finally, Me: In third place is you. Your career. Your own self-interests. No more me, me, me. If you truly put God first and your family second, you will likely find that you are doing great and most other things won't matter to you like they once did.

So maybe it is time to change things around a bit. Reorganize your friends list. Think about your current relational priorities and see if they match up with what God intends them to be.

Priorities are what we make them. It is up to us. We have free will. When you make the "He, we, me" concept the primary importance in your life, things will fall into place.

Just wait and see.

But seek first his kingdom and his righteousness, and all these things will be given to you as well. Matthew 6:33

Since, then, you have been raised with Christ, set your hearts on things above, where Christ is, seated at the right hand of God. Set your minds on things above, not on earthly things. For you died, and your life is now hidden with Christ in God. When Christ, who is your life, appears, then you also will appear with him in glory. Colossians 3:1–4

Chapter 11

Let Go of My Ego

I was recently yelled at by a client. I sat there on the phone with my eyes wide and my jaw open because, my goodness, it was hard to hear what she had to say. She accused me of withholding pertinent information from her when it came to advice on a loan pre-qualification I had given about six months prior. She called me every name and every swear word that was ever invented and then proceeded to tell me how dumb and unethical I was. So that was nice.

While none of what she said was true, I just sat there and listened. I didn't react the way that I wanted to. Trust me, it took *all* of my might. Fifteen years ago, I would have yelled back and would have been very offended. The old me would have argued with her and would have done everything in my power to prove her wrong.

In reality though, that would have caused more conflict and suffering. I quickly realized that her anger really had *nothing* to do with me. She was mad at herself for making a mistake. By not reacting to her attack, I was able to quickly uncover what was really going on and the yelling started to dissipate. She calmed down and apologized.

It could have gone very differently. I also could have taken that bad thing that happening to me and let it ruin my day. Even worse, I could have let my anger and ruin others' as well.

Remember: Good and bad things don't happen to you. They are all merely *things,* and they have a purpose, if you listen and act. Sometimes, they are random things and sometimes God orchestrates to help you learn and grow. He teaches that you have the ability to react and respond in any way you choose. That is your human superpower. Tap into it. Your ego is your kryptonite. When you take something personally, thinking everything is about you, it is the ultimate form of self-importance. Wrong. Nothing is about you.

Your choice, your power is your response to such things. We all have a choice—How will you respond to what comes your way?

Do you want to feed the dark or feed the light? When you react to things with negativity, fear, anger, angst, or victimhood, you make the darkness even darker. When you accept and react to darkness with light, the darkness becomes light. It is that simple.

You choose your reaction and response, and you have the power to create a new future. You must embrace the unknown with the knowledge that you are truly capable of handling everything that comes your way, if you change your mindset. When you get rid of the expected reactions ingrained into you since childhood, you don't *have* to feel fear. You are fully capable of letting go what you *think* you know so that you can grow.

What is the purpose of your suffering? Why is this happening to you?

It is all ego, and your ego has a hard time not being the center of attention. You are not your ego. The ego can be a jerk. You have to stop giving your superpower away to your ego. When you realize that you are indeed separate from your ego, your superpower grows exponentially. You can choose your responses.

It is how God designed all of us. His grand design. Humans have a choice.

To love or not.

To accept or reject.

To be in darkness or light.

Which will you choose?

Fools give full vent to their rage,
but the wise bring calm in the end. Proverbs 29:11

Do not be overcome by evil, but overcome evil with good. Romans 12:21

Chapter 12

Here's Your Sign

Gratitude. The simple action of being thankful in both good and bad times has changed my outlook and my disposition in life. When I started thanking God for His blessings, I soon realized just how favored I really was. Anyone can do this, and you should totally try it.

Today, I want to take it a step further and really get you (and me) to think about things that we don't always think about because we take them for granted.

I have a sign in my house, one of my favorite quotes, which says: "What if you woke up today with only what you thanked God for yesterday?" That got me thinking this morning . . . *Am I really thanking God for all that I should?*

What if I woke up tomorrow with no parents?

No brother?

No husband?

No dogs?

No house?

Water?

Clothes?

Coffee?

Career?

Food?

I should be thanking God for so much more than I am now. Waking up one day without any of the above would be troubling. So why am not actively thanking God for them every single day?

So today, I ask God to open my eyes to be truly aware of the miracles and gifts that He has put before me. At the end of each day, let me recount my many fortunes, no matter how big or small. Let me live each day with compassion, clarity, courage, awareness, love, and thanksgiving. When I lie down to sleep, let me search my heart to recount all of my gifts along the way that day so that I truly understand the magnitude of how undeniably amazing life is.

Thanks God.

The Lord has done it this very day;
let us rejoice today and be glad. Psalm 118:24

Always giving thanks to God the Father for everything, in the name of our Lord Jesus Christ. Ephesians 5:20

Chapter 13

On Aging

Now that I am in my mid-40s, my body is really starting to change.

Last night I went to bed with *no* gray hair in my eyebrows. Zero.

This morning, when I looked in the mirror, there was a stinkin' one-inch thick, gray hair growing sideways out of my brow. How does this happen?

How do gray hairs have the ability to grow at light speed and then pop up in the most unlikely (and unsightly) places? I mean, it takes about a year for my regular hair to grow a few inches, but those gray hairs have super abilities. Jerks.

Don't get me started about growing hair in places where hair has never been. One day nothing is there and the next day, a forest in a place where it just should not be! Hormones!

Wrinkles play the same tricks. One day none, and the next day I look in the mirror and marvel while wondering, *When did those get there?*

This getting older stuff is definitely not for the weak. It makes me laugh most days, but on others, I feel ambushed.

The best thing we can do for ourselves as we get older is eat right, keep moving, and have a good balance in our lives when it comes to stress, spirituality, play, and work. These things will help keep us feeling younger for longer.

We also have to accept the inevitable truth that we will get old one day. There's nothing we can do to stop it.

Michael always tells me I just have to accept it. I chuckle and tell him I will . . . with tweezers and Botox in hand.

Today, when you look in the mirror, focus on what makes you beautiful. When you smile, look lovingly on the wrinkles that appear in the corner of your eyes. Realize that you have earned those bad boys and if you hadn't spent a lifetime smiling, you wouldn't have them.

Do not cast me away when I am old;
do not forsake me when my strength is gone. Psalm 71:9

Gray hair is a crown of splendor;
it is attained in the way of righteousness. Proverbs 16:31

Chapter 14

Just Keep Moving

I f you stop moving, you die!" Those words were an answer from a retired Army General in his early nineties. My question to him was, "What is the best advice you can give me on aging?"

He still played tennis a few days a week, rode his bike on occasion, and lifted weights almost daily. He wore a fedora, loved bowties, smoked cigars, and drank whiskey. My favorite part about him though besides the fact that he was so cute, was how he referred to his wife. She was *my sweet Mary* to him. He told me he called her that from the day he met her.

I had done a mortgage loan for him a few years back and he had taken a liking to me. From time to time we would sit and have lunch and he would fill me with his incredible wisdom on business, love, life, and balance. Lessons that I will never forget.

On that particular day, he elaborated and told me that when a lot of people get older, they think they hurt too much to keep active. He figured out that once he started moving around, the hurt went away and after he got warmed up for the day, he was good to go. He still had muscle tone, walked without a cane, and was resolute and unhesitating.

So that is my thought for the day, for all of us to remember. Just keep moving. You can use this in any aspect of life, really. Keep moving.

She sets about her work vigorously;
her arms are strong for her tasks. Proverbs 31:17

Therefore, strengthen your feeble arms and weak knees. Hebrews 12:12

Chapter 15

Love and Respect

will follow you to the ends of this earth, she thought to herself
and smirked. Who would have ever thought she would feel this
way? She was following him around like a puppy right now and
loving every second of it. Every time he turned around on the
trail they were hiking, he smiled, and she melted.

She finally just let go. Let go of constantly being the domi-
nant one and let her man lead. She submitted to his leadership
and let him be the man. It felt good.

It wasn't something she had done before, this letting someone else lead thing. She never trusted anyone enough to do this.
You would think that this would have been a huge red flag, but
she was blind to it because she didn't believe in it. Didn't feel
like she should. She has always been the boss both at work and
at home. It was her thing. Relationships never ended up well
though because you can't have two masculine forces in a relationship. God made man and woman, and in every relationship, there has to be one masculine and one feminine. You can't
have the same personas, or it won't ever work. It is how we were
designed to be. She took a deep breath in because she realized,
and was now thankful, that it took her almost forty-five years to
figure it out. Perfect timing.

She realized that she didn't always have to be the strong one.
The fixer. The problem solver. The bread winner. The commander. She could lean on him and trust him to do these things for

her. He appreciated this and it empowered him to do more and love her better.

She found that she was free. She felt more feminine. She had feelings and emotions she had never really experienced . . . had never _felt_. The weight she had been carrying was finally off her shoulders. She took another deep breath in and exhaled loudly just thinking about all of it. Then, another smile swept her face.

When she stopped resisting, showed him respect, and followed his lead, their relationship changed.

Respect was key. It naturally led to liberating him to be a better and stronger leader. He loved feeling like a protector and provider, like the head of the household, the _man_.

She figured out that men need respect, so she gave it to him. Willingly and unconditionally. It is more important than love to them, she surmised. As a woman, she found that concept really hard to understand at first. However, when she demonstrated her reverence for him, he began to show her more love. He dotes on her constantly and displays more love as each day passes. He truly loves her, and she _feels_ it. She both respects and loves him. Respect first though.

The more respect she showed, the more she respected him. He felt it and it inspired his love to grow as well.

She smiled again to herself as she silently hoped that other women would figure this out. Every day in her work, she sees the dynamics of how husbands and wives treat each other. She sees the contempt and the aggravation. It is quite obvious why, now, as she has recognized the root cause of their problems. She pays attention to how they talk to each other, and it is the same every single time.

Every once in a while, though, she sees the perfect harmony. She has no problem asking the couples what their secret is. They always just look at each other and smile. They got it.

It is the way that we were designed to be. God knows what He is doing. Promise.

However, each one of you also must love his wife as he loves himself, and the wife must respect her husband. Ephesians 5:33

In this same way, husbands ought to love their wives as their own bodies. He who loves his wife loves himself. Ephesians 5:28

Hiking in Sedona, AZ after a beautiful first snow.

Chapter 16

Those Million Little Things

The little things are actually big things, because those are the things that we miss the most when someone is gone. A laugh, a habit, a saying, even how someone made coffee can become the most treasured memories.

It is not the big gift or the epic vacations that matter. The little things become big, and the big things become small. It's a matter of perspective.

When I climb a mountain, it helps put the world into perspective. When I look down from the top of the mountain, I see a beautiful landscape all as a single view. In reality though, it is a culmination of a million things coming together to create something beautiful.

It is Michael whispering to me after an amazing day, "I don't want this day to end." It is the warmth I feel from his calloused hand. It is the memories I have from childhood of my brother and I jumping in bed with my mom and taking turns scratching each other's backs. It is time spent with my dad talking.

It is holding hands in the car, a hug on a bad day, and feeling the love from the dogs snuggled up next to me. It is our morning prayers and reading God's Word together. That is the stuff that matters.

As I sit here and write this, I am trying to think back to past Christmas and birthday gifts. I cannot remember them most part. I bet you probably can't either. See my point?

I can, however, close my eyes and picture my mom's goofy texts in the morning, my hubby's laugh and those sweet things he said to me a year ago.

We *think* we want those big gifts or over-the-top experiences, and those are great, sometimes. However, that is not what you will miss once that person is gone. Today, take time to appreciate the little things in your everyday life and stop seeing them as little things. They are indeed big things.

Give thanks to the Lord, for he is good;
his love endures forever. 1 Chronicles 16:34

How beautiful on the mountains
are the feet of those who bring good news,
who proclaim peace,
who bring good tidings,
who proclaim salvation,
who say to Zion,
"Your God reigns!" Isaiah 52:7

Chapter 17

Huh, I Wasn't Listening

About a year ago, I wrote the following words in my devotional: When you worry, you think about the past and the future. Live in the present moment now!

That sentiment was a perfect reminder to me this morning as my mind wandered, thinking about disturbing news I had just read. Once I read the news, my mind can hardly help but spiral into a thousand what-ifs.

Michael had just finished reading the devotional to me and I didn't hear a thing he said except for the last part because I remember writing it last year. My mind was on the future. I was worrying.

Instead of enjoying the precious moment of love and fellowship I should have been having with my hubs, I squandered it, on stuff that probably won't ever happen. What a waste of our most precious resource, time.

When I caught myself, I paused. I was doing what the devil wants us to do. He planted that seed, and I was watering it. So I stopped it. I let that seed dry out and die right then and there.

I resolved to live in the present moment, listen to God's Word, and give my full attention to Michael. A calm came over me as he patiently re-read the devotional to me.

In His most perfect timing, the whole page of the reading was about being present with God.

"Therefore I tell you, do not worry about your life, what you will eat or drink; or about your body, what you will wear. Is not life more than food, and the body more than clothes? Look at the birds of the air; they do not sow or reap or store away in barns, and yet your heavenly Father feeds them. Are you not much more valuable than they? Can any one of you by worrying add a single hour to your life?" Matthew 6:25–27

Choices Help You to Be a Light

As we close out this first section, my prayer for you is to realize how important our everyday decisions are. In everything you do, seek His will first before anything else. Pause for just a moment and ask yourself: What would God want me to do? If it aligns with His word, then carry on. If it doesn't, then you know what to do.

Part 2

Be a Light

*"At times our own light goes out and is rekindled
by a spark from another person. Each of us
has cause to think with deep gratitude of those
who have lighted the flame within us."*

– Albert Schweitzer

Our world is in need of more lights. Can you imagine? I believe that some of the brightest lights shine from those who have felt the most darkness. Your light can help brighten the lives of everyone around you.

So let it shine!

Chapter 18

You Bring People to Life

recently returned from a wonderful family visit. We celebrated Mother's Day and my mom's 70th birthday. It was a beautiful time spent with those I love so very much.

I went to see my grandmother, who is now in a nursing home. When I walked in, an aide was there trying to help her into her chair. When she saw me, relief came over her face. I could tell gram was being ornery and I would be able to rescue them both from each other. The aide left us and then it was just gram and me. All was calm. I helped her into her chair, as she can no longer walk by herself.

Gram was overcome with emotion throughout my time with her. When it came time to leave, it was really difficult to do so. I could tell her mind was having a lot of trouble dealing with what she was feeling. Happy I was there. Confused as to why she was there. Trying to remember simple things while processing complicated emotions. Her mind had become so childlike, and it made me feel such profound love for her, it is hard to even put into words. It was powerful. I could feel the whirling going on in her mind.

I could see in her eyes that she knew who I was but could comprehend little else except for the strong emotion of love towards me too.

I just sat there and talked to her and told her how strong she was. She told me she was scared. She just would look at me and start to cry. I told her stories of how she had made it through so many things in her 93 years on earth and that this would be her next hurdle. She had to accept what is even though she didn't understand it.

For Mother's Day, I gave her some lotion, and I offered to rub it on her dry legs, feet, and arms. She said, "You would do that for me?"

I put her leg gently upon my knee, took off her shoe and sock and began to give her a massage. Her smile beamed, and she kept telling me how heavenly it felt. Her skin had become so dry and uncomfortable, and the lotion—along with my loving touch— was welcomed by her.

I remember when I was in the hospital for a while. I hadn't been touched for quite some time. My mom put lotion on my legs and feet, and I remember how amazing it felt. I wanted to return the favor. That little act of kindness was so greatly appreciated, and it was something I never forgot.

I think that most people take for granted those small luxuries in life because we can do them when we are well, but when someone can no longer touch their own feet or rub lotion on themselves, we owe it to them to help do that for them out of love and kindness. Remember I said that. It will come in handy one day. The power of touch is remarkable.

Back to my story . . .

When I was done with her legs and feet, I moved onto her arms and hands which were now mere skin and bones. I don't even know the words to describe how I felt. The realization hit me of what it will be like when I am old and frail. The other part of me realized that her time left on earth was closer to the end than I wanted it to be. As an adult, I have become very close to my gram, and it broke my heart to see her like this.

It was an act of love from me to her and at the end of it, she was crying once again. She looked at me and said, "Jennifer, you bring people to life. That is what you do."

As I write this, I am crying, but when she said it, I stopped, smiled, and cried with her. I got up and gave her a big hug. She gave me the greatest compliment I have ever received.

She then insisted that I help her stand. So I did. She wanted to hug me. So we hugged. I held her so that she wouldn't fall, and she hugged me as hard as she could. She kept on kissing me and squeezing me as hard as she could. I could tell that she didn't want to let go. But she had to.

It soon became too hard for her old bones to keep standing so I gently lowered her back into her wheelchair so she could rest.

She followed me to the door to watch me walk down the hallway as I left. She wanted to get up and give me a hug and so we did one last time. Tears and smiles in both of our eyes, we hugged once again.

I turned around about halfway through my departure and saw her cute little head peeking from the doorway. I love you, Gram.

Consider therefore the kindness and sternness of God: sternness to those who fell, but kindness to you, provided that you continue in his kindness. Otherwise, you also will be cut off. Romans 11:22

"In everything I did, I showed you that by this kind of hard work we must help the weak, remembering the words the Lord Jesus himself said: 'It is more blessed to give than to receive.'" Acts 20:35

Gram insisted that I help her stand so she could hug me.

Chapter 19

A Hug for a Stranger

Yesterday, I thought I had left my sunglasses at a restaurant. My mother-in-law and I had gone there for lunch before an absolutely fabulous spa day. When it was time to head home, three hours later, I could not find my sunglasses anywhere. I tore everything apart looking for them, a total dump everything out of my purse kind of search.

So I went back to the restaurant and asked them about my sunglasses, and they joined the search. I stepped to the side, by the bar and noticed a woman sitting in the corner, wiping tears from her face. She looked sad and I could tell she was having a hard time keeping it together.

Part of me thought, *I need to mind my own business.* However, I felt a stronger tug telling me to go talk to her.

So I went over and asked if she was alright. She looked up at me, surprised, and said, "Yeah, I am okay. Just having a rough day today. Do I not look okay?" I told her that I thought she looked sad. She said, "Yes."

I looked her in the eye and asked if she needed a hug. Surprised once again, she hesitated and then said, "*Yes*!! Badly."

And so I hugged her, a stranger. It was a good hug and I could feel that she needed the encouragement. She hugged me back and started crying, but when the hug was over she had a smile on her face.

"I needed that!" she said. She then went on to tell me she was in the midst of closing out her parents' estate, as both had died recently. She had moved all of the stuff out of their house and now needed to figure out what to do next. She said she knew it was just stuff but the finality of it made her so very sad. She was grateful for our hug.

Just then, the hostess came back with some bad news for me: no sunglasses. I was okay with it though. *I'll just buy another pair*, I thought.

So the lady and I walked out together. We were parked two cars away from each other. She had a smile on her face and told me that my energy brought her great peace. She was grateful for my friendship, albeit if only for a brief moment.

She waved and smiled as she pulled out of the parking lot. My heart was warm, and it was right then and there that I realized what God had done. He put me there right when it mattered. This was His perfect timing. He gave me the courage to embrace a complete stranger without apprehension.

I am glad I listened to Him. I was there to help her and give her comfort. Thank you, Jesus. I am glad I listened.

This morning, I found my sunglasses in the pocket of my purse. I know I looked there multiple times yesterday. I have to laugh. Okay, God.

You never know when you can make a difference in someone's life. There are so many different things that could have happened. I could have ignored her out of fear of being turned down or thinking I need to mind my own business. I kept feeling such strong emotions and the pulling of my heart. I knew it had to be the Holy Spirit.

So the next time you have a compelling need to talk to or even hug someone, you should follow through with that feeling and do it—even if it is a complete stranger.

If you are ever wondering what God can do for you—*through you*—the answer is, anything He wants. He talks to us all of the time; we must learn to listen and act.

But the Advocate, the Holy Spirit, whom the Father will send in my name, will teach you all things and will remind you of everything I have said to you. John 14:26

Trust in the Lord with all your heart
and lean not on your own understanding;
in all your ways submit to him,
and he will make your paths straight. Proverbs 3:5–6

Now may the God of peace, who through the blood of the eternal covenant brought back from the dead our Lord Jesus, that great Shepherd of the sheep, equip you with everything good for doing his will, and may he work in us what is pleasing to him, through Jesus Christ, to whom be glory for ever and ever. Amen. Hebrews 13:20–21

Chapter 20

You Might Not Be Able to Change the World, but You Can Change One Life

Not everyone can change the world, but *all* of us can help change one life.

You never know the impact your words, your actions, or your generosity can make in someone else's life until you actually act. Say or write kind words of encouragement, accolades, and positivity to those around you. Give a hug. Help someone in need. Give someone a chance. Donate generously, even when it hurts.

Open your heart and listen to God's nudges. Trust me, they are there. He has been and will continue to put it on your heart to make that call, do that thing, or pen those words. We just need to be still enough to listen.

I have learned that God's nudges come in the form of chills. I get a thought and then immediately I get chills. This is my sign. I remember when it first started happening. Many times, I chose to ignore the pesky signs because the truth was that I didn't feel like doing what I was being beckoned to do. It was too hard, or I was too lazy. I wonder sometimes how much of an impact I could have made if only I had listened.

Listening, *truly* listening, can be a daunting task. Let's be real here. It is even more difficult to listen when the signs and prompts come at inopportune times. It is not always a convenient time to listen to God. I know I am not the only one who experiences this. It is so easy to ignore His nudges when we are too busy or distracted with our passions and the amusements of the material world surrounding us.

Trust me when I say this: God talks to *all* of us! Yes, even you. Yes, every single day. God speaks to us through signs, thoughts, interactions with people, signals, demonstrations of love, and strong feelings to do certain things. Like I said earlier, I get thoughts that won't go away followed by chills and goosebumps. Sometimes, He smacks us on the side of the head. I have been there, too!

I could tell you countless stories of successful people who were given a chance at some point early in their career, like a new suit bought for them when they had nothing or a word of encouragement that jumpstarted the belief that they could accomplish their goals. It is easy to imagine the difference a hug given when someone feels all alone or rent given when someone is unable to make ends meet can make. I could go on and on. The cool thing is that these people have continued to pay it forward in their lives by doing the same for others. That, my friends, is what God wants us to do. Make a difference in one person's life and you can impact so many others exponentially.

The point is this: You have no idea how much you can impact the life of another, but God does. There are so many pivot points in everyone's life, where one decision, one act., one word can change the course of a life. When that happens, the future of so many others can be altered too, for generations. It blows my mind to think about such things. It is true though.

Let God work through you. Allow His thoughts to enter your mind and your heart. Let Him work His miracles through you and you will see your efforts become contagious.

It is easy to give up on doing good because you don't think a small gesture can make a difference. You would be wrong though. You, my dear friend, have the ability to change the world one person at a time.

———————————————◆———————————————

Therefore, my dear friends, as you have always obeyed—not only in my presence, but now much more in my absence—continue to work out your salvation with fear and trembling, for it is God who works in you to will and to act in order to fulfill his good purpose. Philippians 2:12–13

"I am the true vine, and my Father is the gardener. He cuts off every branch in me that bears no fruit, while every branch that does bear fruit, he pruned so that it will be even more fruitful. You are already clean because of the word I have spoken to you. Remain in me, as I also remain in you. No branch can bear fruit by itself; it must remain in the vine. Neither can you bear fruit unless you remain in me." John 15:1–4

Chapter 21

Power in the Pause

While lifting weights a few days ago, a thought came into my head: Pausing at the top of the rep makes you get stronger. Pause, squeeze, and release.

Later, I found myself becoming irritated with something at work. My first inclination was to shoot off a response or react with anger, but I paused and took some deep breaths enabling me to then respond in a much nicer way.

When leaving for a meeting, I consciously paused all throughout the day without understanding why I was doing it. Before I responded to anything, I paused, and then I reacted.

I discovered I was doing it in a myriad of ways, from taking a short walk, to deep breathing, to praying for a minute before reacting. When I fully realized what was happening, I laughed a little. God was talking to me big time.

There is power in the pause—in pretty much every aspect of life.

Think about it.

A pause makes you stronger. It gives you more insight. It makes you kinder and more understanding. It gives you rest and temporarily stops you from operating in autopilot. Autopilot is real. We all have habitual responses that we give without thinking, but if we would pause for a moment, the response would be different—it would be better.

This concept and example is even in the Bible! James 1:19 says, *"My dear brothers and sisters, take note of this: Everyone should be quick to listen, slow to speak and slow to become angry."*

We all need to pay attention to the pause. Try it and experience the peace it brings into your life and to the lives of those around you.

For the Spirit God gave us does not make us timid, but gives us power, love and self-discipline. 2 Timothy 1:7

Chapter 22

Give it Away, Give it Away, Give it Away—Now!

The greatest joys I have had in my life have come from giving generously to others, even when I had little to give.

It has been said that in order to keep something, you have to give it away. That, my friends, rings truer than you would ever think—until you experience it for yourself. I love giving stuff away!

I remember experiencing this phenomenon in my early 20s. I had $200 left in my checking account, and I gave $150 of it to a friend in need. I did it without thinking and also without realizing through the ramifications of only having $50 to live on until my next payday.

Within a few days, I started receiving unexpected checks—a refund for one thing, an overpayment for another. Within a few more days, over $500 was in my account. Back then, that was a huge deal. God provided for me. That's how it works.

As my career and success has grown, so has my desire to give to others. Few things are more satisfying to me than helping others. I love to be able to make a difference in someone's life, either through experiences or lending a helping hand.

I know how it feels to have nothing. I have been there. I was also on the receiving end of someone else's generosity, and it impacted my life. Maybe you've had a similar experience.

In order to be successful, you have to pay it forward. You have to give without expectations. Your actions must be open-handed and freehearted. Not only do you have the ability to change someone's life, but yours will change as a result.

Need more reasons for why you should be generous?

You should spread the love. Give back as a thank you for all of the blessings you have been given. Use your privilege as a way to bring hope to those who have none. Charity and generosity provide a good example to others to motivate them to do the same. Giving inspires giving. It is good for your soul and for overall peace. Helping others creates a stronger sense of community. You will be happier, healthier, and more grateful.

Give because you can. Everyone can. No matter what. Every single one of us has the ability to make an impact. When you give, you will be rewarded in return. God is cool like that.

"Give, and it will be given to you. A good measure, pressed down, shaken together and running over, will be poured into your lap. For with the measure you use, it will be measured to you." Luke 6:38

Each of you should give what you have decided in your heart to give, not reluctantly or under compulsion, for God loves a cheerful giver. 2 Corinthians 9:7

Chapter 23

Well, Maybe You Can Change the World

I recently received an unexpected letter from a colleague. He thanked me and let me know that my words of encouragement propelled him to take the next step with his business. He is now extremely successful in his part of the business world.

I am definitely not taking credit for his success but read on and you will see my point.

I thought back to our conversation about a year and a half ago and I don't remember saying anything profound, I just offered encouragement and shared some things I had been afraid of and then conquered when I first arrived in San Antonio. I thought I was simply sharing my honest opinion about what I thought his abilities were. We talked about keeping God in the middle of everything. I told him I saw him being the biggest and best at what he did because his vision was to truly help others versus to make a lot of money. To him though, my advice and listening ear helped him keep going.

Side note: When making money is your *only* motivation, I believe your success will be short lived. Love what you do and if you happen to make a lot of money doing it, consider that a perk.

His letter got me thinking about how powerful the words we tell ourselves and speak to others are. You might not think you can make a difference in someone's life, but let me assure you, you already are.

So which words will you choose?

Anxiety weighs down the heart,
but a kind word cheers it up. Proverbs 12:25

With the tongue we praise our Lord and Father, and with it we curse human beings, who have been made in God's likeness. Out of the same mouth come praise and cursing. My brothers and sisters, this should not be. Can both fresh water and saltwater flow from the same spring? My brothers and sisters, can a fig tree bear olives, or a grapevine bear figs? Neither can a salt spring produce fresh water. James 3:9–12

Set a guard over my mouth, Lord;
keep watch over the door of my lips. Psalm 141:3

Chapter 24

Don't Be That Person

Recently, while driving home, I witnessed a car desperately and hurriedly trying to get around other cars in traffic. The people around him took it upon themselves to self-regulate his driving. They were purposely trying to stop him from passing and getting around them. It was like a game to them, a power-play. We've likely all been guilty of it. We don't want the other person to win, so we block their attempts at passing us so we feel better about ourselves—or something like that.

I hung back, watched, and thought to myself, *Who are we? Why do we take it upon ourselves to judge what this person is doing? What if he is trying to get to an emergency? What if something just happened?*

You see, I have been the crazy person weaving in and out of traffic, getting regulated by others. What they didn't know was that I was frantically rushing to my mom's house because something had happened to my stepfather. Another time, my dog was dying, and I was rushing to the vet to say goodbye before it was too late.

The point is, you have no idea what is going on in someone else's life, why they are driving too fast or whatever. It could be that they are rude and selfish, or it could be that they are in a critical situation.

Either way, just get out of the way, and don't take it personally. It is not for us to judge. Unless they are acting in a way that is radically dangerous (If this is the case, call the authorities.), let them be.

"Do not judge, or you too will be judged. For in the same way you judge others, you will be judged, and with the measure you use, it will be measured to you. "Why do you look at the speck of sawdust in your brother's eye and pay no attention to the plank in your own eye? How can you say to your brother, 'Let me take the speck out of your eye,' when all the time there is a plank in your own eye? You hypocrite, first take the plank out of your own eye, and then you will see clearly to remove the speck from your brother's eye. Matthew 7:1–5

Chapter 25

Grudges Are Dumb

It makes me sad to say this, but half of my family on my dad's side don't talk to each other. It might be the same with your family too. It really stinks for us non-grudgers because we get to be in the middle of the destruction that the grudge holders have caused. I originally wrote this for them to read, but I feel like others could benefit from what I have to say here.

If your family is like mine and you are stuck in the middle, you will fully understand what I am saying below. If you are a grudge holder, listen up because I am about to tell you important information that you have selfishly disregarded.

Life is too short to hold grudges. Grudges keep you in the past and hold you back from enjoying the moment that you should be in, which is the present.

Not one person has ever benefitted from holding a grievance against someone. No problem has ever been solved. No healing has been had, only a lot of hurt, and the biggest hurt comes to yourself.

Holding onto anger creates anxiety, depression, and stress within your body. It weakens your immune system and affects your health both physically and mentally. You perpetuate your own suffering.

Oh, and you also affect those around you. You affect your family and friends. Estrangement limits when you socialize, and it also makes get-togethers awkward because other people have to plan around your problem. You alienate your friends and family because you are holding onto something from the past, not to mention the fact that an angry, bitter person isn't much fun to be around.

I believe that when people hold a grudge, it is a way to establish an identity of victimhood. They feel they have been wronged. Or, they think they are right and you are wrong and to prove that point, they allow themselves and others to suffer. Good going.

I get it, you got hurt. You were wronged. You were treated unfairly, perhaps betrayed. So you decide to hold a grudge. What good does it do anyone? Exactly.

I encourage you to think about a few things if you are holding a grudge right now. Take a step back and look at yourself.

- What good has come out of it?
- How has it impacted your life?
- How can you expect God to forgive your sins if you don't forgive the sins of others?
- Have you ever tried to see both sides of the situation?
- Have you tried to sincerely reach out and give a heartfelt apology even though you might not be entirely at fault? Remember that forgiveness is just as much about you as the other person.
- Acknowledge your feelings and work through them and then *let it go*—even if the feeling is not reciprocated.

When you truly seek the answers to these questions, pray about them, and ask God to take those negative feelings away from you. Surrender. Have grace.

Remember, your time on earth is short, too short to be tainted by the destruction that a grudge can cause.

Each heart knows its own bitterness, and no one else can share its joy.
Proverbs 14:10

*And when you stand praying, if you hold anything against anyone, forgive
them, so that your Father in heaven may forgive you your sins.* Mark 11:25

A gentle answer turns away wrath, but a harsh word stirs up anger.
Proverbs 15:1

*Do not be quickly provoked in your spirit, for anger resides in the lap of
fools.* Ecclesiastes 7:9

*Do not repay anyone evil for evil. Be careful to do what is right in the
eyes of everyone. If it is possible, as far as it depends on you, live at peace
with everyone. Do not take revenge, my dear friends, but leave room for
God's wrath, for it is written, "It is mine to avenge; I will repay," says the
Lord. On the contrary: "If your enemy is hungry, feed him; if he is thirsty,
give him something to drink; In doing this, you will heap burning coals
on his head." Do not be overcome by evil, but overcome evil with good.*
Romans 12:17–21

*Then Peter came to Jesus and asked, "Lord, how many times shall I
forgive my brother or sister who sins against me? Up to seven times?"
Jesus answered, "I tell you, not seven times, but seventy-seven times.*
Matthew 18:21–22

*Get rid of all bitterness, rage and anger, brawling and slander, along with
every form of malice. Be kind and compassionate to one another, forgiving
each other, just as in Christ God forgave you.* Ephesians 4:31–32

Chapter 26

The Gift

The year 2006 was rough for my family. My grandfather passed away from a very long and drawn-out illness leaving my grandmother alone for the first time in over fifty years.

I wanted to do something special for my grandma that year, so I decided to give her a very unique gift. I thought of 100 questions I had always wanted to know about her, like: What is a perfect day for you? or How did you pick out your first home? and Talk to me about one of your favorite memories with your sister. I also bought her little gifts that I thought would make her smile. I wrapped them and gave them all numbers. I then cut out each question and pieces of paper for the numbered gifts and put them in a decorated jar. I also gave her a journal to write all of her answers in.

Her instructions were simple: Take one piece of paper out of the jar each day and follow the instructions on it. Sometimes she had to write and sometimes she could open a gift. I thought it was the perfect gift to give her as it was the gift that kept on giving!

She loved it and at first, she would call me a lot to talk about the questions and to let me know she was following her instructions.

It eventually dropped off and she didn't talk about it anymore. I thought that maybe she just stopped doing it and I decided not to bring it up. Years passed, and my gift became a distant memory. Honestly, I completely forgot about it.

When I went back home to Buffalo, NY for a visit a few years ago, (she was ninety-one at the time) guess what she gave me? You guessed it, the journal! Turns out she had completed it all those years ago. She had misplaced it when she moved into her home and had finally found it. She could not wait to give it to me!

I have read through the questions she answered many years ago. She taped them to the journal and then wrote her answers on the page. Most have made me laugh, but I have also cried. She really wrote with all of her heart. She was honest and transparent, and she wrote the most beautiful things about some people that were in her life. A great deal them are no longer with us.

What a treasure this book is. I now know more about my grandma than I ever have. How she thinks. How she felt about things. The way things were for her during the depression. How she grew up. Her favorite things. We can learn so much from our elders.

All of it is so very beautiful. It was a gift alright, but it ended up being a gift from her to me instead.

Fast forward to today, my grandmother has dementia and she is in a nursing home. When I pick up the journal, it reminds me of who she once was, a vibrant, first-generation Italian woman with a whole life of adventures before her—adventures that are now recorded for myself and my family to read forever because I took the time to ask.

If you are reading this, I would encourage you to do this for someone in your life. You will not regret it.

Do not cast me away when I am old;
do not leave me when my strength is gone. Psalm 71:9

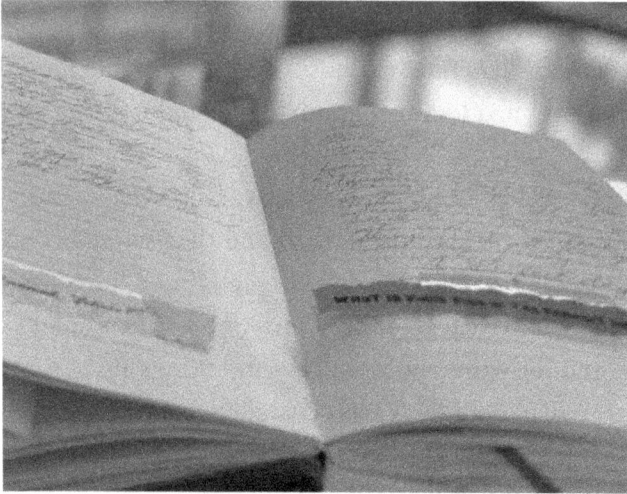

My treasured gift. I forever have my grandmother's memories and thoughts.

Chapter 27

It Is Good, It Ain't Perfect

I used to have a problem with perfection. If whatever I was doing wasn't perfect in my estimation, I just wouldn't do it. It was all or nothing. No messiness or weakness was allowed. Everything had to be immaculate and flawless.

When I lived in Dallas, I got gussied up just to go to the grocery store. Now, stuff like that makes me laugh. *If old me could just see me now . . . Ha!*

I felt like no one could know my deficiencies and to be vulnerable would mean admitting my failures as a person. I wasted a lot of good years.

God's creation was originally made perfect, but we blew that in the garden. Now, we are all flawed whether we admit it or not.

So why do we let our pursuit of perfection keep us from becoming the best version of ourselves right now?

Is the frozen pizza thrown in the oven with great company better than the fancy dinner we never cook at all?

Is the thirty-minute workout better than the one-hour workout we could not do?

Is a simple gesture of love better than buying a gift you never give?

Is the five pounds lost better than the twenty you didn't?

With walls up and masks on, we lie to each other about our deficiencies. We are in pursuit of perfection in everything we do so much so that we forget how sweet it is to go just go with you got. To enjoy right now and stop accepting the latter of the above.

I want to make a fancy dinner, so I will do it next week instead of tonight.

I will be happy when I lose twenty pounds, so I won't celebrate my five and just give up.

I can't work out for an hour today, so I won't bother.

You get it.

What about how we want everyone to think we lead perfect lives? Boy, is that a lot of work!

We are perfect! Nothing wrong here to see. Keep moving on. Don't get too close.

Why don't more of us tear down these walls? Or better yet, why do we build them to begin with? Be real. Be vulnerable. Be *very good,* not perfect!

I think that we believe we can't be truly loved unless we are perfect (or appear to be). So we hide the stuff that makes us . . . us. It makes no sense!

Peace isn't going to come from keeping your walls up and your mask on every day. Peace is going to come when you strip off the tightly wrapped sheath you have all around you. It is about having your head held high as you cry, "This is me! All of me! The good and bad parts (and the parts that I am ashamed of!). This is who I really am, and God loves me this way and so do I. I am no longer worried about what anyone else thinks because I know I am good enough."

Not perfect.

If you are still looking for perfection, you can experience it in His perfect love for the imperfect you. You can hear it in His perfect Word. You can find it in His perfect sacrifice for you.

*Indeed, there is no one on earth who is righteous,
no one who does what is right and never sins.* Ecclesiastes 7:20

*No one has ever seen God; but if we love one another, God lives in us, and
his love is made complete in us.* 1 John 4:12

*For by one sacrifice he has made perfect forever those who are being made
holy.* Hebrews 10:14

Chapter 28

Fix Your Thoughts

I know a lot of people who are angry because they have the news on 24/7. I used to be one of those people. I have since turned off the television. There's always something to be irritated with. You don't have to look so hard nowadays. It is easy to feel agitated right now given the current state of this fallen world we live in.

The negative energy buzzing and colliding right in front of us is causing people to be unsettled and quite edgy. People have had enough, and just when you think things can't get worse, something else happens.

What do we do? I was really feeling it this morning, even without the news on. So I asked for a sign. I do that sometimes. I ask God to show me what He wants me to see. Most often, He does.

Today, He showed me something I had written a few years ago in my *Jesus Calling* book. I wrote, "Fix your thoughts on Jesus and He will fix your thoughts."

As soon as I read it, I smiled. Aha! It really is that simple.

When we fix our thoughts on God, He *will* change the way we think. It is inevitable.

Jesus has our back. He keeps our paths straight. He takes our burdens. He lifts us up. He heals us. He gives us peace. He is always there for us.

Feelings of fear, anger, worry, and distrust dissipate when we fix our eyes on God. When you refocus your thoughts on what is good, right, noble, true, honorable, and just, a feeling of contentment and calm will permeate your body and penetrate your soul.

So today, when you look out into the world, look up instead and smile. God is right there with you. He's got you.

You will keep in perfect peace
those whose minds are steadfast,
because they trust in you. Isaiah 26:3

Fixing our eyes on Jesus, the pioneer and perfecter of faith. For the joy set before him he endured the cross, scorning its shame, and sat down at the right hand of the throne of God. Hebrews 12:2

Fix your thoughts on God and He will fix your thoughts. A view from the top in Sedona, AZ.

Chapter 29

Men Are Not Dumb, No Matter What the Television Says

I recently watched television (like with commercials and every-thing!!) while on vacation. Within minutes, I was quickly reminded of something that drives me crazy, as it should you too. Commercials and shows portray men as a bunch of wusses. Stupid men. Weak men. Men who would not be able to survive without a woman who is *way, way* smarter than him.

What is up with that? Why aren't more people speaking up about this?

Do you not think that it is subliminally brainwashing those who watch? It is teaching young minds that men are too dumb to do anything. They are providing a platform for a systematic breakdown of self-worth in boys. Showing them false assumptions. You don't think that this will mess up minds? Gender roles? It does.

So why are they doing it? I racked my brain on this one and I don't get it. Is it the feminist or girl power movement? Is it over-the-top politically correct compensation (like, they are so anti-traditional that they have gone the complete opposite just to prove a point)?

My advice is this: When you are with your kids and a dumb guy show or commercial comes on, say something. Defend men.

Assure them that men are not stupid. Tell them that what they are seeing on television is not true. Give them opposite examples of what they are seeing. Be a good example yourself.

Then maybe turn off the television.

For the husband is the head of the wife as Christ is the head of the church, his body, of which he is the Savior. Ephesians 5:23

"Then you will know the truth, and the truth will set you free." John 8:32

Do not conform to the pattern of this world but be transformed by the renewing of your mind. Then you will be able to test and approve what God's will is—his good, pleasing and perfect will. Romans 12:2

Chapter 30

Make Your Home
Your Sanctuary

With the exception of a beautiful hiking trail, my home is my sanctuary. It is a place of peace and calm. It is comfortable and filled with things I think are beautiful, things I love and things I have collected over the years. Pictures. Memories. Smiles. Love.

When I come home from work, spent, I absolutely love coming to *my* home because it calms me. I know that my dogs will be waiting for me, wanting me to get on the ground with them so they can jump on me and kiss me. I know that it will be chaos, free and warm. I know I can wrap myself up in a blanket and enjoy a glass of wine outside on the back porch.

I keep it well maintained, neat, and clutter-free for the most part. It's comfortable and not too fancy. I have made it to fit me.

This is important stuff here. All of us need our own sanctuary, somewhere we can come home to that we have actually made into our *home*. We need a place to calms us, comfort us, and bring us peace.

I think back to my childhood and how chaotic it was. Growing up with an alcoholic father, we never knew what each day would bring. Home was not a place of peace. I hated being home back then. Home was a place of being scared and always on guard.

Maybe that is why it is so super important to me now.

Living in chaos is not healthy and I wonder why so many people actually choose to do it to themselves. Unless you are a child and cannot help it, we all have within us the ability to create our own individual home somewhere in our lives—a place where we feel safe, secure, and calm.

It could be a room, a location, an actual house. Just make somewhere your home.

You won't regret it.

For God is not a God of disorder but of peace—as in all the congregations of the Lord's people. 1 Corinthians 14:33

When you lie down, you will not be afraid;
when you lie down, your sleep will be sweet. Proverbs 3:24

Chapter 31

I Pray for You. And You. And You.

Have you ever had one of those days where everyone drove you thoroughly nuts? Of course, you have. I have too. Every. Single. Day.

Here's a cure I have discovered which always puts a kybosh on that attitude. Ready for it?

Pray for every single person you see (especially the ones who are annoying you). It doesn't have to be a long prayer. Pray for their happiness and wish them well. Pour God's blessings upon them. Smile.

"Huh?" I can just hear you say that now. Trust me, it is possible, and it will make it almost impossible to be a hater.

When you are having *one of those days* or even if you are not—pray for others that surround you. Your attitude will change. Your light will shine. The world will be a little brighter.

Try it!

I urge, then, first of all, that petitions, prayers, intercession and thanksgiving be made for all people. 1 Timothy 2:1

In the same way, the Spirit helps us in our weakness. We do not know what we ought to pray for, but the Spirit himself intercedes for us through wordless groans. Romans 8:26

Chapter 32

Things Above—Share
Your Testimony

How do you share what it is like to have a living, breathing relationship with God?

I think a lot of people feel awkward when it comes to sharing the good news about Jesus. Some go about it the wrong way. You can't be forceful about it. Think about what you do when someone tries to force something on you. You run the other way.

God wants us to share Him with those we meet, but so many of us don't do it because we are either too scared or don't know how.

I had been asking God to show me how to best do it and in true God form (for me), I had a vivid dream. When I woke up, I smiled and laughed a bit because it all came to me perfectly. An allegory for sharing Jesus.

Here it is. . . .

There is a department store called, "Things Above" and everything in it is free. All you have to do is show up and start taking all of the wonderful things the store has to offer. Your cashier is Jesus. He waits for you and greets you with a smile when you walk in.

The first thing you have to do before taking home the gifts He has to offer though, is make an exchange. You exchange your old self for a new self. Once you put on your new self, there are a few other things to exchange.

Jesus is happy to take them back even though you didn't buy them at His store. He has a great exchange policy.

With you is a suitcase you've been dragging around—for pretty much your entire life. It's heavy, and it has been a burden keeping it with you wherever you go.

Once you have your new self, ridding yourself of that suitcase is the next priority. So you go up to the counter and take out one object at a time to hand over to Jesus. He takes each one and exchanges it for something better.

You hand Him doubt and He gives you trust.

You hand Him addiction and affliction and He presents you with aversion and alleviation.

You hand Him your burdens and He gives you encouragement in return.

Chaos is swapped for peace and shame for unconditional love.

One by one, your suitcase gets emptied. You realize the gifts Jesus gave you don't weigh a thing and it makes you smile.

Soon, the suitcase is completely empty, and you don't need or want it anymore. Why would you? You give it to Jesus and He tosses it in with millions of other empty suitcases.

You feel so much better and wonder why you didn't do this before. Now, it is time to shop!

Aisle by aisle, you see the coolest stuff on the shelves, and it is all free. Belts of Truth, Armor of God, Breastplates of Righteousness, Shields of Faith, Helmets of Salvation, and Swords of the Spirit, and they all fit perfectly. You also pick up some kindness, patience, and a lot of forgiveness and grace. Smiling big, you still can't believe all of this stuff is free. You want to kick yourself for not doing this sooner. Then, you realize the timing was actually perfect.

As you leave, you stop by and say, "Thank you" to Jesus once again for all of these amazing gifts. You ask Him how long the store has been in business and He answers, "Oh, about 2000 years." He then winks at you, smiles, and adds, "Come back any time. I am always here when you need me."

Now that you are home, everyone—I mean *everyone*—is noticing your new digs. Plus, you aren't carrying around that ridiculous heavy suitcase anymore. Your friends and family, who are still dragging theirs around, want to know what you did. So you share the story about Jesus and what He did for you.

Because that is the natural thing to do.

If people want to know what a relationship with Jesus is like, I tell them about who and how I was before versus who I am now. For those who have known me long enough, they can see it without me saying a word. They notice my light, and people will notice yours too.

It doesn't matter who you are or what you have done, Jesus died for your past and your future. May you have the courage to share your testimony.

Neither do people light a lamp and put it under a bowl. Instead they put it on its stand, and it gives light to everyone in the house. Matthew 5:15

Then Jesus came to them and said, "All authority in heaven and on earth has been given to me. Therefore go and make disciples of all nations, baptizing them in the name of the Father and of the Son and of the Holy Spirit, and teaching them to obey everything I have commanded you. And surely I am with you always, to the very end of the age." Matthew 28:18–20

May you have the courage to share your testimony.

Chapter 33

Strangers

I feel like no one raises their eyes to meet others' anymore. Instead, faces are either buried in their phones or down toward the ground ahead of them. I try and read the faces of others and it makes me sad. Oh, how the world would be so much better if people would just look up.

If we keep our heads down, people can't see the hurt in our eyes or the anxiety plaguing our endeavors. Or maybe we've become so disconnected, the mere thought of looking someone in the eyes fills us with trepidation. I don't know.

I like to play a game with myself when in crowded areas like airports or busy streets. I look up and try to get people to look back at me. When they do, I smile at them. Most times they smile back, but sometimes I think people become unnerved, thinking, *Who is this person looking me in the eye?* It is like they don't know what to do! It is one small way of connecting with those around me and showing them a little love, even when they aren't expecting it. It makes me feel more human. There is so much more to life than looking at your phone.

I feel like the connection, albeit for a brief moment, actually helps people. Deep in all of our hearts, we want someone to notice us, and when you look at someone in the eye, it shows that they matter enough to do so. I respect you. I see you. I love you.

So the next time you are walking down the street, look up and smile.

Open my eyes that I may see wonderful things in your law. Psalm 119:18

For the entire law is fulfilled in keeping this one command: "Love your neighbor as yourself." Galatians 5:14

Chapter 34

Power in Prayer

I believe one of the bravest and most spectacular things a person can do for another is pray for them . . . right in front of them.

When you are on the receiving end of it, the power and potency can be overwhelming. It might make you feel uncomfortable at first, but once you get past that, you feel the effects and never look back.

God puts it into our hearts to commune with Him on behalf of other people. "I'll pray for you" is something that we tend to say a lot, but do we *actually* do it? I think that most of us do not. Lip service doesn't serve anyone.

My challenge for you is this: Next time you say it to someone, make good on it right then and there with them. See what happens. At first, it will be scary. I assure you though, there are no bad prayers. Don't worry about messing up.

When you do it, your love will radiate. God's light will shine through you and a sense of peace will fill *both* of your hearts. The Holy Spirit will guide you.

Keep your heart open. Be vulnerable. Be bold. You won't ever regret it. It might mean everything to the person that you are praying for.

Words carry so much power. They have the ability to change lives and heal broken hearts. Let someone know you care enough about them to not give two cares about what anyone else around thinks.

Don't think you can do it? I assure you, you can. Pray to God to give you the tenacity. He will.

Therefore, strengthen your feeble arms and weak knees. "Make level paths for your feet," so that the lame may not be disabled, but rather healed. Hebrews 12:12–13

Therefore confess your sins to each other and pray for each other so that you may be healed. The prayer of a righteous person is powerful and effective. James 5:16

Chapter 35

When the Christmas Lights Go Out

Who doesn't like to see the sparkles and glimmer of Christmas lights? The shimmering and twinkling in the midst of a dark of night have a way of bringing a sense of calm and childlike wonder to us, no matter our age.

I love to walk throughout the neighborhood and look at all the trees and homes lit up. I adore seeing Christmas trees in the windows as I pass by.

Taking all of this in, brings me happiness. It is my favorite time of the year. It might be yours too! Part of me wishes we could keep the Christmas lights up all year, but then I think it would ruin the magic. Too much of a good thing, I suppose.

Last week, during one of my early morning walks, I noticed it was dark, too dark. I realized quickly that the Christmas lights were no longer up. My world of dancing lights and incandescent wonders came to an abrupt end. I wasn't ready! I needed more time!

The world returned to normal once again, and I had to console myself with the thought that they will be back next year. To me, Christmas lights are magical. They create the anticipation and joy of something spectacular to come. They symbolize love, spending time with your family, Christ's birth, parties, laughter, and generosity towards others. They illustrate a time when we look for ways to be nicer, more forgiving, and softer toward others.

When the lights go out, I feel like they go out in people's hearts also. Wanting people to "Keep Christmas in their hearts" is such a profoundly true statement. If we could only keep those internal lights on all throughout the year.

As this section of the book comes to an end, let this chapter be a reminder for you to keep your Christmas lights on a little longer this year. May you continue to be a light in the world.

In the same way, let your light shine before others, that they may see your good deeds and glorify your Father in heaven. Matthew 5:16

When Your Light Shines Bright, You Will Overcome

When we have God in our hearts, our paths will become clear. They might not be easy though, and that is okay. Most things worth doing aren't easy anyway. Let that grit and gratitude take over and show the world it doesn't matter who you are or where you come from. Jesus calls all of us to be strong in Him. That means you too.

Part 3

Overcoming Your Past Does Not Dictate Your Future

"We must learn to live on the heavenly side and look at things from above. To contemplate all things as God sees them, as Christ beholds them, overcomes sin, defies Satan, dissolves perplexities, lifts us above trials, separates us from the world and conquers fear of death."

– A.B. Simpson

We *all* have a past. It is time to leave it right there and stop letting what happened control who you are now as a person.

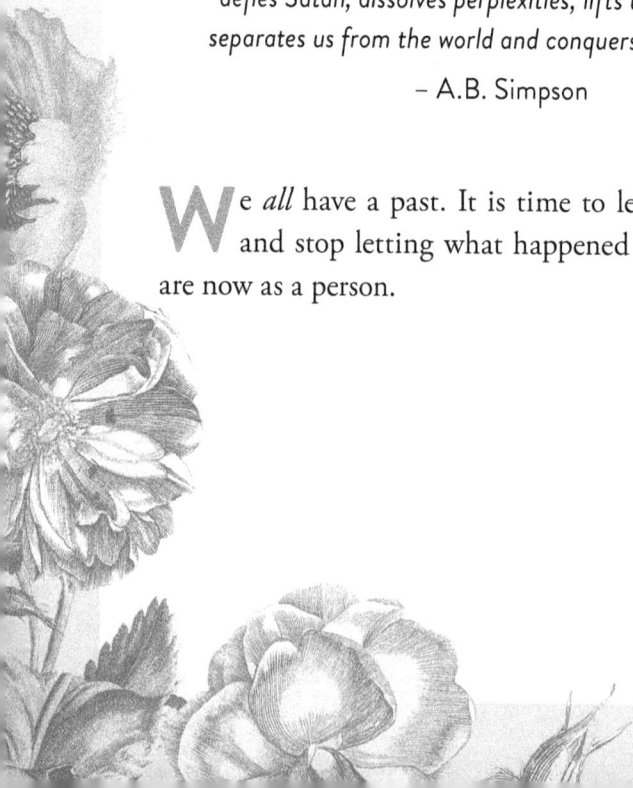

Chapter 36

The Giant Rock Split by a Really Large Tree—A Corny but True Metaphor for Life

While hiking once, we came upon a giant tree that had split a huge boulder into two pieces. It made us pause for a moment and we joked about the tree being a great metaphor for life and overcoming obstacles.

Once, that tree was just a seed on top of a big boulder. When the seed began to grow roots, it came upon a small crack in the rock. Despite its overwhelmingly unfortunate circumstances in which its little life started, the seed persisted. It grew and grew. The branches reached to the sky and its roots pushed into the rock harder and harder. Millimeter by millimeter, the tree grew, and it did not let its environment dictate its future. Instead, it persisted daily until it was strong enough to crack the boulder in half.

It was no longer captive to the rock. The tree grew into its full potential.

We can do the same, you know. Small changes every day. We need to gaze up to the sky and plant our roots to stand firm. Day by day, we get stronger and overcome our own obstacles to break whatever rock is keeping us from fulfilling all God has planned for us.

Small changes equal big results.

"Have I not commanded you? Be strong and courageous. Do not be afraid; do not be discouraged, for the Lord your God will be with you wherever you go." Joshua 1:9

Whatever you do, work at it with all your heart, as working for the Lord, not for human masters, since you know that you will receive an inheritance from the Lord as a reward. It is the Lord Christ you are serving. Colossians 3:23–24

He replied, "Because you have so little faith. Truly I tell you, if you have faith as small as a mustard seed, you can say to this mountain, 'Move from here to there,' and it will move. Nothing will be impossible for you." Matthew 17:20

The tree that persisted daily and split that rock in two.
If a tree can do this, imagine what you can do.

Chapter 37

Turn It Off and Slow Your Roll

I have been guilty of numbing. Heck, there have been points in my life where I just didn't *want* to deal with the reality the direction my life had gone, so I kept doing a bunch of nothing. I would drink too much wine, watch endless TV, or keep my phone glued to my face because doing so was easier.

It took me a while to dig out of that hole. Living like that was tough, and it takes a lot of gumption to deal with the things we don't like about ourselves.

Here are my thoughts:

Turn off the television, your cell phone, and the endless things keeping you distracted from what is really going on in your mind—at least for a little while. Or maybe it is mind-numbing alcohol or drugs that you turn to instead of dealing with the things you need to feel.

When we look at ourselves in our simplest form, most of us would find that we are not as we should be. Who we really are is not who we portray ourselves to be.

Are we fulfilling what we were born to be or are we settling for something less? Who are you, really?

When we know the answer to this and that answer doesn't align with the truth, we numb. We mask the disappointment or whatever feeling we are trying not to feel because it is easier to remain stuck than to actually do something about it. It is too scary so we numb and distract. We merely get through the day without dealing with anything and then do it again the next day, and then next, and so on.

What a waste of a life.

When there is silence and clarity, we are forced to reckon with those feelings we have. We are forced to find out who we really are and what we were meant to be. In the silence, God speaks to us. We might not love what He has to say—a lot of times, He calls us out on our rubbish. It is okay though.

If we listen, He shows us the life we could lead. We just need to meet Him in the quiet space.

When you do listen and act, there is no turning back because once the light gets turned on, you realize the dingy dark room you've been living in isn't for you anymore. God has something way better than what you've been.

When you are stuck in a rut, it takes a lot of work to get yourself out. So many have the propensity to stay there and be miserable for the rest of their lives. That somehow seems easier to them. It is okay to stay there for a little while because we need to feel hurt and pain. However, it is your job to be better. God is there to help you do just that if you let Him.

Jobs you hate. A settled relationship. Friends who really aren't friends. Someone you need to forgive but still hold a grudge against. Resentments. Lies. Victimhood mentality. Low self-esteem. Anger. Jealousy. Laziness. Such is not how or who we are supposed to be. Numbing and distracting ourselves would be a monumental waste of this beautiful life. We are so much more. We can do so much more.

It is, "Be still and know that I am God." It is not, "Distract thyself with a whole bunch of junk so you don't have to deal with who you really are." Got it?

Make the most of your gifts from God. He will show you what they are, but you have to actually do something about it. Feel the feelings. Make the changes. Deal with things. You got this.

My son, if you accept my words
and store up my commands within you,
turning your ear to wisdom
and applying your heart to understanding—
indeed, if you call out for insight
and cry aloud for understanding,
and if you look for it as for silver
and search for it as for hidden treasure,
then you will understand the fear of the Lord
and find the knowledge of God.
Proverbs 2:1–5

The one who enters by the gate is the shepherd of the sheep. The gate-keeper opens the gate for him, and the sheep listen to his voice. He calls his own sheep by name and leads them out. When he has brought out all his own, he goes on ahead of them, and his sheep follow him because they know his voice. John 10:2–4

Be still before the Lord
and wait patiently for him;
do not fret when people succeed in their ways,
when they carry out their wicked schemes.
Refrain from anger and turn from wrath;
do not fret—it leads only to evil.
For those who are evil will be destroyed,
but those who hope in the Lord will inherit the land.
Psalm 37:7–9

Chapter 38

My Dad Was an Alcoholic, and It Helped Me Be Successful

I grew up with an alcoholic father. This has helped me in the business world. It could have gone the other way. However, I used my superpowers for good instead of letting myself remain a victim.

What did I learn? I learned how to read people and their facial expressions. I learned how to analyze body movement because I had to anticipate what was going to happen.

Out of survival when I was young, I become a master at it. I had to learn things a child should not have to because nothing in my life was certain. I had to feel a room, the house, the voice in order to figure out what was going on. What kind of mood was he in? What should, or shouldn't, I say so as to not get smacked, belittled, or punished? Of course, I hated it, but it taught me many things.

I learned to tell what I was in for from footsteps alone.

I figured out at a very young age that if I used these skills, I could avoid bad interactions. As I grew up, I started using them in other areas of my life. I read people. I could feel what they were feeling and quickly understood their wants and needs.

It is one of the reasons for my success as an adult. Turns out those skills come in pretty handy when dealing with other people in business.

So many people become a victim and use instability as an excuse for their current unproductive state or failures. You don't have to. No one does.

I don't know what your childhood trauma is, but I do know that you don't have to be a victim. Learn from it. Become stronger through it.

Turns out, God used my volatile childhood and turned it into something good, just like He always does. I only had to let Him. Good can always come from bad.

The survival skills I learned back then have come in remarkably handy as an adult. I attribute much of my success to it.

So it is all good. Thank you, God. I learned how to forgive, how to anticipate, and how to duck and swerve. I learned how to have thick skin and get over stuff quickly, how to cook my own food, and how to be self-sufficient. It all worked out for the best because allowed it to by bringing God along with me for the ride. I am grateful.

Now, my father stopped drinking over 10 years ago and he is truly a changed man. I hold no grudges from the past and have forgiven him completely.

What do you need to let go of from your past? It is time. Think about something negative from your childhood and contemplate how God has used it to make you better.

And he who searches our hearts knows the mind of the Spirit, because the Spirit intercedes for God's people in accordance with the will of God. And we know that in all things God works for the good of those who love him, who have been called according to his purpose. For those God foreknew he also predestined to be conformed to the image of his Son, that he might be the firstborn among many brothers and sisters. Romans 8:27–29

Then Peter came to Jesus and asked, "Lord, how many times shall I forgive my brother or sister who sins against me? Up to seven times?" Jesus answered, "I tell you, not seven times, but seventy-seven times." Matthew 18:21-22

You intended to harm me, but God intended it for good to accomplish what is now being done, the saving of many lives. Genesis 50:20

Chapter 39

Almost Dying so I Can Live

I t is hard for me to believe that three years ago, I was dying. Literally. I had massive blood clots in both my lungs and my heart was failing. I was days away from no longer being on this earth.

I had blacked out from lack of oxygen, and I got out of breath just trying to talk, yet I was in such denial of the 453,636 signs of blood clots that I chose to ignore them all. You would think I would have learned the first time, but I almost didn't.

The doctors told me that if I had waited one more day to get to the ER, I would have died. "God was certainly watching over you. You must be here for a reason," they said.

I believe that to be true, and I thank God most every day for the profound blessing I have been given—my life. My recovery has been nothing short of a miracle.

When you are confronted with your own mortality—for me three times now, blood clots twice and then cancer—you change. Everything is different. I mean *everything.* You look at each day, each lesson, and each experience radically different.

You figure out what is important and what is not. What is worth getting angry over and what to let go. You appreciate more. You become more grateful. You love better. You forgive quicker. You smile more. A light goes on in the inside of you and it keeps you remembering what could have been.

Life is so much better. Extraordinary, actually. It is weird to say this out loud, but sometimes I wish more people could have the same experience, so they would appreciate the very short time we have on earth. Almost dying propelled me to live my life as God has intended me to. Imagine a world in which we all lived that way.

When I was a child, I talked like a child, I thought like a child, I reasoned like a child. When I became a man, I put the ways of childhood behind me. For now we see only a reflection as in a mirror; then we shall see face to face. Now I know in part; then I shall know fully, even as I am fully known. And now these three remain: faith, hope and love. But the greatest of these is love. 1 Corinthians 13:11–13

Teacher, which is the greatest commandment in the Law?" Jesus replied: "'Love the Lord your God with all your heart and with all your soul and with all your mind.' This is the first and greatest commandment. And the second is like it: 'Love your neighbor as yourself.' Matthew 22:36–39

"Martha, Martha," the Lord answered, "you are worried and upset about many things, but few things are needed—or indeed only one. Mary has chosen what is better, and it will not be taken away from her." Luke 10:41–42.

Chapter 40

You are Here, Aren't Ya?

The fact that you are reading this now proves you have survived your worst days. They have passed and yet you are still standing here. We are made up of the cumulation of our worst days and our best days. They have shaped us, and we are victorious.

That was actually my waking thought yesterday and it proved to be the theme for my day.

The morning started out with my computer not working. I had to drive into the office and have the IT people fix it. The incident put me about two hours behind. I hit every traffic light, got behind every slow person, and went through three school and construction zones. My frustration rose.

When I got home, the computer still had problems. So I called IT and they remotely accessed the computer to try and fix it. I had the emails I had taken care of minimized so I could close them as I finished my tasks . . . and every single one of them disappeared! By then, I had over twenty voicemails, fifteen text messages, and now another 100+ emails I had to go through. I get about 500 per day. My self-imposed stress level was at its tipping point and the emails disappearing set me over the edge.

I had a meltdown and cried. Yeah, the almost 45-year-old superstar loan officer cried. I totally freaked out, until I realized that I just needed to start praying. So I did. I asked God to bring me peace and calm, as well as direction and patience. He did.

I calmed down and laughed at myself as I started to redo my to-do list by searching through every single one of my emails to find the ones that required my attention. I had to take a big gulp of my own advice. It worked though. Thank you, Jesus.

You see, that waking thought I had, was a definite premonition of things to come and it was a great reminder that each challenging moment will pass. It is inevitable.

I had to control my reaction because it was the only thing I had control over. When I sat back and took a deep breath, I realized that my response needed to change. Through prayer and giving my burden—no matter how trivial—to God, He brought calm to me.

I got most of my work done. Phone calls returned. Emails replied to. Problems solved.

My lesson for the day was a gentle reminder of, "This too shall pass." No matter what you are going through right now—whether a small thing like mine or something much more profound—use your past to prove to yourself that you will get through this too.

Today is a new day. I learned a great lesson. It doesn't get much better than that.

There is a time for everything,
and a season for every activity under the heavens:
a time to be born and a time to die,
a time to plant and a time to uproot,
a time to kill and a time to heal,
a time to tear down and a time to build,
a time to weep and a time to laugh,
a time to mourn and a time to dance,
a time to scatter stones and a time to gather them,

a time to embrace and a time to refrain from embracing,
a time to search and a time to give up,
a time to keep and a time to throw away,
a time to tear and a time to mend,
a time to be silent and a time to speak,
a time to love and a time to hate,
a time for war and a time for peace.
Ecclesiastes 3:1–8

Therefore, we do not lose heart. Though outwardly we are wasting away, yet inwardly we are being renewed day by day. For our light and momentary troubles are achieving for us an eternal glory that far outweighs them all. So we fix our eyes not on what is seen, but on what is unseen, since what is seen is temporary, but what is unseen is eternal. 2 Corinthians 4:16–18

You will surely forget your trouble, recalling it only as waters gone by. Job 11:16

Chapter 41

On Independence

Afew years ago, I broke both of my ankles while hiking in Costa Rica. My girlfriend and I had hired a guide to take us on a remote hike about an hour south of Nicaragua. It was a ten-mile, out-and-back trail that ended in a beautiful huge waterfall in the middle of nowhere. Along the first five miles of the hike, we saw a lot of monkeys, deer, and colorful birds. The guide commented to us that the creatures were acting strangely and unusually wild.

The good news is, we made it to the waterfall. It was incredible. On the way back though, there was a 6.7 magnitude earthquake. We were about 100 miles away from the epicenter.

It started with a roar and then the rolling ground reared its scary head. The trees and the landscape swayed back and forth as if on top of stormy water instead of land. If you have ever been in an earthquake, you know what I am talking about. It was scary. We froze in awe because we didn't have anywhere else to go.

Once the main quake was over, we started heading back to the trailhead 4.5-miles away. I wanted to get the heck out of there, so I started hiking back quickly. The jungle was dense, and the trail was covered with unstable rocks and roots. In the sunlight beams shining through the trees, I saw what I *thought* were horseflies on our narrow trail. It turns out . . . they were not.

I walked smack dab into a nest of black wasps whose nest had gotten moved after the quake. Within seconds, I was covered in wasps. The guide, who saw what was happening to both my friend and I, shouted, "RUN!!!!"

We did. Trying to get those wasps off of us while running as fast as we could caused me to fall. To be honest, I didn't even know I had hurt myself until I finished punching the last wasp off of me. I knew I had been stung many times, and I thank God neither of us are allergic because none of us had an epi pen or a satellite phone.

When I tried to get up, I realized I was hurt pretty bad. The problem was that we were still four miles away from the trailhead. They could not carry me as the trail wasn't wide enough for even two people to go through, so I had to walk the whole way back with two broken ankles. I didn't know they were broken at the time though. I thought I had at the very least torn every ligament in both my legs. It was a very slow walk. I am pretty sure I made it with God and pure adrenaline pumping through me.

My trip home from Costa Rica was awful. I remember crying on the plane because I was in so much pain. I didn't have casts yet and instead was wrapped in Ace bandages all the way up to my knees. I could not walk on my own feet and was in a wheelchair.

My mom picked me up from the airport and drove me home, so I could rest in anticipation of my appointment with the orthopedic doctor the next day. When I arrived home, my husband (now ex-husband) had decided to move out . . . and take all of the furniture with him with the exception of my bed and desk.

I wanted to crawl up in a ball and disappear. I sat there alone and cried and cried.

On Monday morning, my father came down from Buffalo to help take care of me. I found out I had broken both of my ankles. I was going to be in double casts and a wheelchair for a long time. It ended up being twelve weeks in casts and twelve more in fracture boots.

While the above is the crazy part of my story, the rest of this chapter is the *real* story. It is the story of getting close to my father . . . and my Father.

For the first few days, I was really angry. I became the ultimate bed witch—because I couldn't do a thing—to my father who was just trying to help me.

My dad and I had kind of a sordid past. Our relationship when I was younger was a little tumultuous at times. He and I weren't close. As time has passed, we have worked on our relationship a lot and are very close now, which is awesome.

I was a jerk, having a pity party for myself because I had lost all of my independence. Someone had to take care of me, and I didn't like it one bit. I could not do *anything*. Close your eyes and imagine having two casts on your legs. Think about any daily activity and imagine what could and could not be done with casts on both legs. It stunk.

One particular night, during the epitome of me feeling sorry for myself, I snapped at my dad when he tried to move my pillow under my legs. I cried myself to sleep that night because I no longer was self-reliant. All I could think about was everything I could not do, and my attitude only got worse.

I finally fell asleep. Then I began to dream. God had something important to tell me.

What I remember is being in the dark and hearing a voice. I wasn't scared but felt at peace. The voice said, *"Jennifer, you had become too independent. I am fixing that for you right now. Now is the time to be dependent on your Father. Let Him take care of you.*

Enjoy your time and build your relationship with your Dad. Don't waste this precious time."

And then I understood.

I woke up crying that morning. This time, it was a cry of joy. I called my dad in, and I told him that I was sorry and that I was so appreciative of him coming to my rescue when I needed him the most. From that day on, our relationship has flourished. I enjoyed every minute of him being there and let him help me. I also worked on my relationship with my other Father.

When I acknowledged my neediness, I grew closer to both God and my father. I thanked God for the difficult time because through it, I realized that my insufficiency was the key to further developing our relationship. Along the way, I discovered all of the beautiful things around me. My injury was a gift, and I am thankful for the powerful lesson. God had His own way of making sure I would actually listen.

My attitude, along with my entire disposition, changed that morning. It also served an additional important lesson about our mindsets that I have carried with me: Your gratitude fixes your attitude. My level of happiness shot up a trillion points that day, not because my experience changed but because how I looked at it changed.

Thank you, Jesus.

So do not fear, for I am with you;
do not be dismayed, for I am your God.
I will strengthen you and help you;
I will uphold you with my righteous right hand. Isaiah 41:10
Many are the plans in a person's heart,
but it is the Lord's purpose that prevails.
Proverbs 19:21

For I know the plans I have for you," declares the Lord, "plans to pros-
per you and not to harm you, plans to give you hope and a future.
Jeremiah 29:11

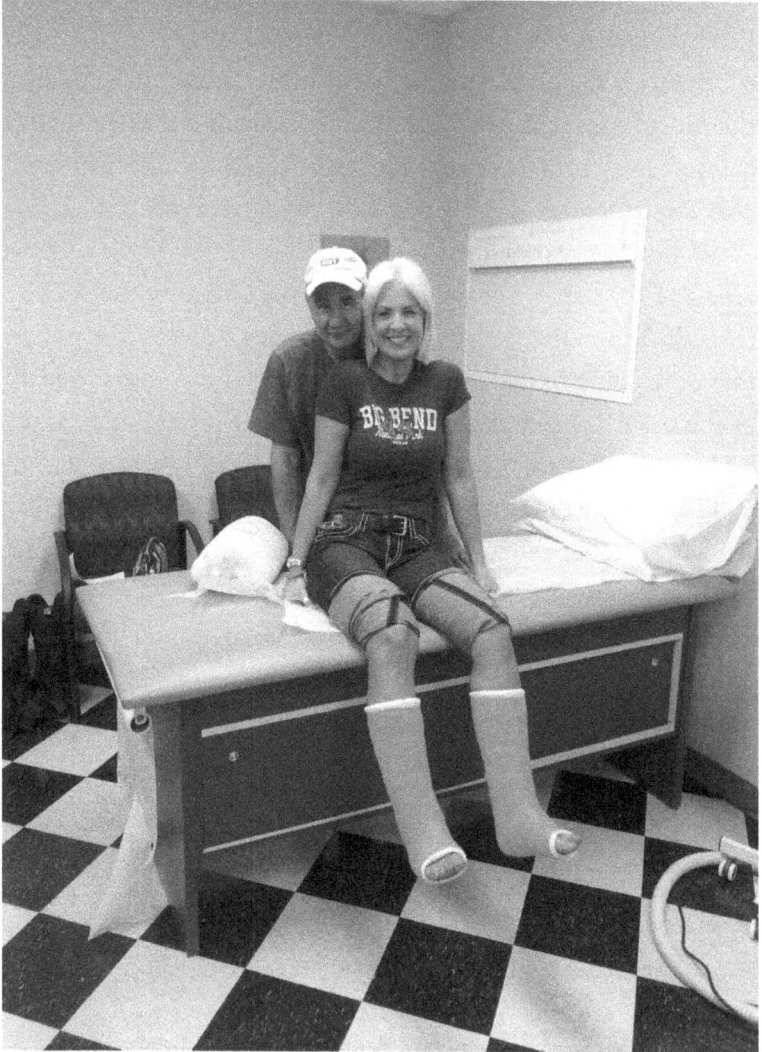

Dad and I with my hot pink casts.

Chapter 42

When You Hurt

On my darkest days, I have cried out to God, "*Why?*" With tears in my eyes and fire in my soul, I have demanded answers that were not for me to know.

When we hurt, we want the rest of the world to stop just like ours did. But it won't.

Have I not commanded you? Be strong and courageous. Do not be afraid; do not be discouraged, for the Lord your God will be with you wherever you go. Joshua 1:9

When we hurt, it feels like the hurt will never end. But it will.

Be joyful in hope, patient in affliction, faithful in prayer. Romans 12:12

When we hurt, we feel like we are alone and no one else knows how we feel. That is not true.

So do not fear, for I am with you; do not be dismayed, for I am your God. I will strengthen you and help you; I will uphold you with my righteous right hand. Isaiah 41:10

When we hurt, we feel sorry for ourselves. We shouldn't.

My comfort in my suffering is this: Your promise preserves my life. Psalm 119:50

When we hurt, we feel helpless and ashamed. We aren't and shouldn't be.

Therefore, since we have been justified through faith, we have peace with God through our Lord Jesus Christ, through whom we have gained access by faith into this grace in which we now stand. And we boast in the hope of the glory of God. Not only so, but we also glory in our sufferings, because we know that suffering produces perseverance; perseverance, character; and character, hope. And hope does not put us to shame, because God's love has been poured out into our hearts through the Holy Spirit, who has been given to us. Romans 5:1–5

You see, God is with you and with me. We work through things because our Almighty God is with us through it all. Not just sometimes but *all* of the time.

I know it feels like you are alone in your suffering. God never promised we wouldn't hurt. What He did promise is that He will be with us *always.*

Reach up your hand to grab His, and go on your journey together.

Talk to Him. Shout to Him. Write to Him. Whisper to Him. He's a great listener. I promise. You might not get all of the answers you seek in the midst of your pain, but you will find purpose in it if you trust Him.

Chapter 43

You Have to Be Tested in Order to Have a Testimony

'm good God. Really. I don't need another test. I have plenty of testimonies. I said those words a few years back while fighting for my life in the ICU. Obviously, I survived, and I am a better person today because of what I have been through.

He brought me through some pretty rough stuff, and if I had the chance to change anything in my life, I certainly would not change my most difficult times. Although they felt awful while going through them, I kept my faith and I kept Him close to me. It was all for a purpose greater than I could ever imagine. His plans were better than mine could ever be.

When stuff happens, we think that we know better than God, especially when hardships come inopportune times. There is never a convenient time to have a personal catastrophe. It will just happen, and we must deal with it.

When struggles hit your life, the *only* choice you do have is how you react to it. You can be a victim, or you can be strong in God knowing that the Mighty Father will be there next to you fighting with you—if you let Him.

For our light and momentary troubles are achieving for us an eternal glory that far outweighs them all. So we fix our eyes not on what is seen, but on what is unseen, since what is seen is temporary, but what is unseen is eternal. 2 Corinthians 4:17–18

Chapter 44

All the Good We Cannot See

Let me tell you a story about my wedding.

We decided to get married in Rockport, TX, and there was a lot of logistical planning involved. Both our families were coming from out of town, and we wanted to make sure everyone was taken care of. The only thing we wanted to worry about when the time came was having fun!

We originally secured a house that could sleep thirty people. It was right on the water with a huge deck on the back where we could hold our wedding reception and ceremony. We were so excited, so we booked it and paid for it in full. Thinking our plans were secure, we made other arrangements for everyone else's lodging and made all wedding plans around that house.

As it turned out, our reservation was cancelled very unexpectedly about three weeks before the wedding. The owners had sold the house, and the new owners didn't want to do an Airbnb anymore! We had to quickly find somewhere to stay and somewhere for the ceremony. Yikes!

I am happy with myself because I did not panic. I dealt with the news and knew that everything would work out for the best.

We found other houses and rented them. We even got lucky and rented a Pavilion on Rockport Beach where we could hold our ceremony and subsequent reception. There was nothing else available on such short notice. The only problem was that the Pavilion was near a small part of the beach, and it didn't have bathrooms or electric hookup so we would have to get generators. We would have to make do with what we had. We proceeded with our plans and worked with the wedding planner to use these facilities.

Then the lady at Aransas County called me and nervously broke the news that they had double booked our pavilion. *Seriously? Now what?*

Maybe it is all of the yoga and deep breathing I had been doing that helped me remain calm, but I remember taking a deep breath and asking her, "Okay, well what are our options?" She went through a long list of things to do that included sharing the space or splitting up where we get the pavilion. After telling her that would not really work for us, she said, "Well, you can have the beachfront pavilion. Someone just cancelled as we speak."

After my own private victory dance, I composed myself and said, "Yes!" This was a pavilion on the widest part of the beach with its own private bathrooms, kitchen, and air conditioning.

It was perfect!

The morning of the wedding, Michael and I took a long walk through the neighborhood, and we walked by the house we were originally supposed to rent. Guess what? The entire deck was under water! A storm surge from the hurricane caused the water levels to rise, so there was no way we would have been able to hold our wedding there.

We just looked up into the sky and smiled. Thank you, God.

It is relatively uncomplicated to see a beautiful sunrise, a majestic mountain, or the trees sway in the wind. The beauty and good we can see is right in front of us.

What about the good that we cannot see? What about the things orchestrated behind the scenes that we don't initially see as good at the time, but really are. Any one of those calamities I described earlier could have been seen as terrible and bad, but as you can see, they were all very good things indeed.

There are things in our everyday world beyond our understanding. It is because our views are dramatically different than what God sees. We see up-close. He sees the whole picture and smiles. *Trust me, my child. I will bring good things out of this. Just wait and see.*

You have to trust the Lord in all situations, not just some. You have to believe that when things happen which are not in our plans or that seem to make no sense to us, there is a greater purpose. He knows better.

When things don't go your way or as you had planned, remember my little story here. Gently remind yourself there is good happening that you cannot see. Sit back, relax, and see what God does.

Trust in the Lord with all your heart
and lean not on your own understanding;
in all your ways submit to him,
and he will make your paths straight. Proverbs 3:5–6

So we fix our eyes not on what is seen, but on what is unseen, since what is seen is temporary, but what is unseen is eternal. 2 Corinthians 4:18

The perfect day and the perfect sunset. God's plans are so much better than ours.

Chapter 45

Second Wind

Whenever I start a hike, for roughly the first half of it, I dawdle. I know . . . shocking for someone who loves to hike so much. I don't know why this happens; it is a struggle.

I don't quite *feel* like putting forth the effort it is going to take to complete my trek. But I do it anyway because I have never regretted it.

Something magical happens halfway into my hikes—every single time. I get a second wind. So much so, I conveniently forget any previous hesitations or exhaustion I thought I had.

This got me thinking . . . a second wind is awesome. I am glad God programmed it into us.

It keeps us going even when we feel we don't want to. It gives us strength when we feel defeated. It puts the wind back into our sails and the skip back in our step.

In life, like in my hiking experience, we venture into many second wind situations. They remind us to keep going.

Do the hard thing. Don't give up. Push through. Proceed with life with renewed vigor because you got this!

God has equipped you with the strength to press on. So press on!

You'll get your second wind.

Let us not become weary in doing good, for at the proper time we will reap a harvest if we do not give up. Galatians 6:9

Therefore, since we are surrounded by such a great cloud of witnesses, let us throw off everything that hinders and the sin that so easily entangles. And let us run with perseverance the race marked out for us. Hebrews 12:1

Chapter 46

I Cairn About You a Lot

I love to hike. Along the trails I traverse, I am guided by cairns that show me which way to proceed. Sometimes, the path ahead of me is not always clear. I need something to show me which way to go, whether I am going in the right direction or on the wrong path in need of redirection. Other times, I *think* that I am on the right path, but a distant cairn tells me otherwise.

When I was hiking recently, the cairns got me thinking about how we need cairns everywhere we go, not just when we hike. Visualize this for a moment and let me show you how these path markers can be applied to our everyday lives.

Your cairns help you find the right direction. They help you from getting lost.

How cool would it be to have our own personal cairns show us where to go and what to do? They would let us know when we are on the wrong path and need to turn around and take a different way. They would encourage us when a path is rough that we are headed the right way and our efforts will be worth it.

Ponder all of that for a moment.

Here's the good news: We *do* each have our own personal cairn to show us which way to go. It is God. It is also the Bible. God plants those guiding lights for us everywhere. We just need to pause, look, and listen. Listen with your heart. Feel His direction with your soul. The only way to do this is to open yourself up to the directions right in front of you. They have always been there, but we've just been too busy to see them, hear them, or feel them.

God took the time to carefully and intentionally place each stone—stones that He knows are best for us—so that our pathway will be balanced. That is what He wants for each of us.

The path we should be on is not always the path that we are on. He lets us know through gentle whispers and tugs at our hearts: "*Wrong way! Go here!*"

If our heart isn't open, we won't see or hear the direction we are supposed to go. We will get lost.

We will take the long way or the wrong way. We will either end up somewhere we aren't supposed to be at all or go to a destination not intended for us. There is a better way, a clearer path, and we don't want to miss it.

My prayer for you today is that you pay attention to the cairns before you. May you pause long enough to see the beacons God has meticulously laid out for you.

May you follow your cairns.

Give careful thought to the paths for your feet and be steadfast in all your ways. Proverbs 4:26

Be alert and of sober mind. Your enemy the devil prowls around like a roaring lion looking for someone to devour. 1 Peter 5:8

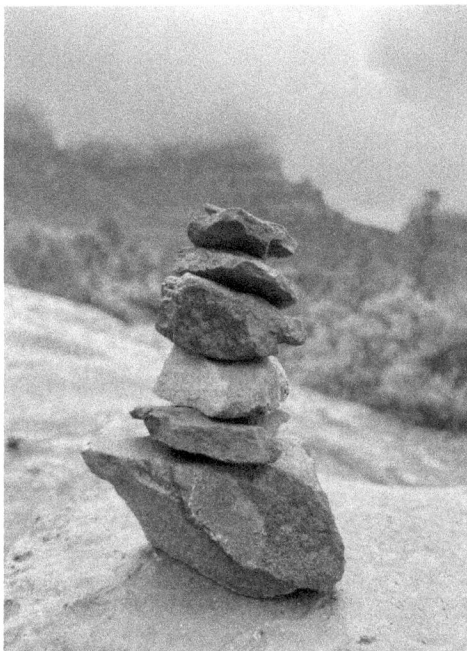

A cairn. May you find your way back when you are lost.

Chapter 47

Butterflies

I always say that butterflies are God's way of telling me, "Everything is going to be all right but prepare for change. It will be beautiful when it's done." Every time I see butterflies, it is in the midst of some sort of cocooning period for me. They start showing up everywhere in my life, and it makes me smile. *Thank you for the reminder, Jesus.*

Butterflies are evidence of what happens when you emerge out of the cocoon that you are in. All of that ugliness in the beginning ends up being worth it when you realize that the tough times are for something far greater and better than you could have imagined.

You have to look at it this way: When you are going through tough times, God envelops you with His most loving arms—if you let Him. He shields you and protects you, just like a cocoon. He stays with you during your metamorphosis because He sees what you will become when your storm is complete.

When it is time for you to emerge, He sets you free and gives you a little push. *It's okay now.* One day, you will look in a mirror and not even recognize the person you once were. The *you* before your transformation is no longer, for you will have become a beautiful butterfly.

Trust the pause you are in and embrace the cocoon, because you know what will happen next!

It was all worth it. Thank you, Father. I get it now. Thank you for keeping me safe.

And we all, who with unveiled faces contemplate the Lord's glory, are being transformed into his image with ever-increasing glory, which comes from the Lord, who is the Spirit. 2 Corinthians 3:18

And have put on the new self, which is being renewed in knowledge in the image of its Creator. Colossians 3:10

Chapter 48

I Used to Be Fat, and I Can Say That Because I Was

I used to be fat, like 100+ pounds larger than I am now. This story is not meant to make anyone feel bad but to show you the power of transformation.

After my thyroid was removed, I ballooned within a very short time—three to four months. It was maddening, saddening, and very difficult emotionally for me. Every day I woke up a few pounds heavier than the day before. I wasn't allowed to take any medicine to regulate my body until my cancer treatments were over.

I remember those days like they were yesterday. Maybe I have PTSD about it still because now I am ultra-careful with my weight. I don't want to be like that again. I felt so horrible both about myself mentally and myself physically.

It took me a long time to lose that weight. I completely changed the way I ate and for the first time in my life, I started to exercise regularly. It was back then that I discovered my love of hiking. Walking was the only thing that I *could* do.

I started off small in the beginning. Slowly the weight came off, and I found that I could do so much more than I had ever imagined. Since then, I have climbed Mt. Kilimanjaro, hiked the Inca Trail to Machu Picchu, hiked down the Grand Canyon to Havasu Falls, climbed Mount Whitney, trekked the

Tour de Mont Blanc, and have conquered many more trails and mountains. Hiking helped transform my innermost self and my outward appearance.

Mentally, I found that it cleared my mind. The sun on my face and shoulders and the crisp air in my lungs brought me renewed happiness and great peace. I discovered that the friendliest and most encouraging people I had ever met were on the trails. Within a few minutes of walking in nature, my stress levels were down, and I became completely focused on the present moment. It is absolutely glorious. I found that I was capable of so much more than I had ever imagined. It rubbed off on my personal life too. I began to transform.

Physically, I got stronger and stronger. I got in better shape and the weight came off. Slowly. It seemed like forever. When you have a lot of extra weight on you, it is hard to keep encouraged when you don't see immediate results. When you are that overweight, you really don't notice five or ten pounds coming off. Anyone who is buxom like this understands the struggle. Then one day you wake up and actually *see* a difference. At that point a light comes on inside and from that day on, it's *I can do this*.

I've been there, and I have overcome. I just had to figure out what kind of exercise I actually liked to do. Showing up was the hardest part in the beginning, but once I was there, I never regretted it. If you have some extra pounds, and you are physically capable of exercise, that is what you need to do: figure out what you would *like* to do and then follow through. As my friend Lisa used to tell me many years ago, "The best exercise for *you* is the one that you will actually do." She was right back then, and she still is now.

Our minds are the main culprits for negativity when we are challenged to do hard things. It can tell us, *You aren't strong enough to do this*, while our bodies secretly know we can do more. Don't let your lazy mind win. Your soul needs to take charge and show your body who's boss.

Working out is a privilege and so is getting stronger. That is the mindset I maintain.

I fell in love with how fitness makes me feel many years ago, and the relationship continues to thrive. It is a way of life. Fitness has saved my life and it continues to propel me forward every day. It keeps my stress levels at bay and brings me peace. There has never been a workout I regretted, ever.

Thank God today for giving us the ability to do the things our minds tell us are too hard. Ninety-nine percent of the time, they are not. You just have to believe and execute. Hiking happened to be the thing for me and it has evolved from there. Now I enjoy may different activities depending on my mood. The point is that I always do *something* to keep moving. You can do the same.

One step at a time. It might never be easy, but it will always be worth it.

Do you not know that in a race all the runners run, but only one gets the prize? Run in such a way as to get the prize. 1 Corinthians 9:24

Do you not know that your bodies are temples of the Holy Spirit, who is in you, whom you have received from God? You are not your own; you were bought at a price. Therefore honor God with your bodies. 1 Corinthians 6:19–20

Chapter 49

Shame, Shame, Shammmmeeeeee

Shame. Shame is a liar. Vulnerably, I will tell you that the skeleton no longer in my closet is the relationship mistakes of my past. When I was younger, I appeared to have everything together in my life, but I sure didn't have my love life in order. The fear I had of others finding out about my past failed relationships stopped me from dating certain people because I didn't want them to think badly of me. I felt deeply ashamed.

As I've gotten older, I have realized that we *all* have our share of things we are embarrassed about and don't want people to know about us—for fear that they will think differently about us.

I don't care who you are, shame can stop all of us from living a life of wholeheartedness because we're afraid of being judged. Instead, we retreat and don't do the things we are meant to do or meet the people we're meant to meet. I learned that when the *right* person comes along in your life, whether a partner or a new friend, they are not going to care about what happened in your past. They will know that your past is what made you into who you are today. They won't judge you for the things that happened before them, rather knowing about your past will enable them to love you in the here and now. It's really that simple.

Do not be ashamed of your past. Learn from it. God loves all the less-than-favorable parts of you that you try to hide from everyone else.

He knows you and He loves you the same. So why do we stop loving ourselves or deem ourselves unlovable because of mistakes from our past? That, my dear friend, is the devil at work. He wants us to feel ashamed. Don't listen.

God sees all parts of you and He still loves you unconditionally. Everyone makes mistakes. There is only one Person in this world who was perfect, and it ain't me and it ain't you!

It is never too late to turn back from bad decisions, to be wiped as white as snow, to repent for past transgressions. All you have to do is ask.

It is that simple. God has forgiven you for all that you have done and now it is time to forgive yourself.

Therefore, there is now no condemnation for those who are in Christ Jesus. Romans 8:1

He answered, "I heard you in the garden, and I was afraid because I was naked; so I hid." Genesis 3:10

Chapter 50

When I Was Sick, Everything Was Clear

In my first book, *The Storm*, I talked about my most recent brush with death. I had massive pulmonary emboli and near complete heart failure. I ended up having to take four full months off work to recover. It was during that time that I was able to write my book, and I am convinced that all of it happened so the book could be written.

I was thinking the other day about true, clear thought. It is the kind of thought that comes with quietude and with truly being still. I had no choice during my hiatus from work because I had nothing else to do for the first time in my life.

Man, did I think clearly. It was beautiful, calming, and freeing. When I finally stopped my brain from paying attention to the clatter, stillness washed over me like a gentle, refreshing rain. It was awesome.

The stress, the worries, the hogwash all melted away. My pause made most everything insignificant and miniscule because I realized that it doesn't really matter. I understood that I was giving too much relevance to things that weren't worthy of my reverence. That is what God was trying to tell me. I wasn't listening before because I was too busy.

That is what my illness did for me. It was a beautiful pause.

I have never had so much peace in my life, and it was incredible. My thoughts were so clear. My understanding was revealed. I had so many ideas and epiphanies. I carry them with me to this day, and I will continue to do so for the rest of my life.

As I sit here and write this, tears come to my eyes because I wish that everyone could feel this. I do believe everyone can.

I believe that those who understand their own mortality are the ones who *truly* live. When you fully grasp the fact that one day you will die, you begin to live your life differently. It's true. Just ask someone who has had a brush with death. You probably won't even have to ask. You can probably already see it. They are different.

The realization and acknowledgment that life is temporary and precious will exponentially grow your satisfaction of the present moment. You will see things differently. You will feel differently. Stuff that matters to a person who doesn't have the insight won't matter to you. Life is too short. The things that do matter to you are the things actually worth caring about. Love. Time. Contentment. Acceptance.

Stuff just won't bother you like it once did. Grudges and long-term resentment won't be worth it.

I take a lot of time each week to meditate, pray, and breathe for a while. I put down electronics and just be still.

My wish for you today is that you take time to realize that pressing pause for a little while is of utmost importance to your well-being. In order to think clearly—I mean *really* clearly—you have to be focused on your intermission rather than your play. The show that goes on all around you will go on, but to appreciate the amazing life God has for you, you have to be still long enough to hear His whispers. Don't miss them.

It doesn't have to be long. Just five to ten minutes a day to just *be* for a bit. It took me almost dying to truly figure it out, but it doesn't have to be that way for you. You can start now.

When you wake up tomorrow, be grateful for another day you have been given. Contemplate the impermanence of our life here on earth. Stop wasting your highly valued time and start living.

Therefore we do not lose heart. Though outwardly we are wasting away, yet inwardly we are being renewed day by day. For our light and momentary troubles are achieving for us an eternal glory that far outweighs them all. So we fix our eyes not on what is seen, but on what is unseen, since what is seen is temporary, but what is unseen is eternal. 2 Corinthians 4:16–18

Consider it pure joy, my brothers and sisters,[a] whenever you face trials of many kinds, because you know that the testing of your faith produces perseverance. Let perseverance finish its work so that you may be mature and complete, not lacking anything. James 1:2–4

Chapter 51

Those Things We Say (To Ourselves)

What do you say to yourself when you look in the mirror? What do you say to yourself when you make a mistake? What do you say when you embark on an endeavor that scares you?

When you feel all alone or when you are forced to stop and think, what are your inner thoughts like? Are you too scared to let them free?

My dear friends, it is the things we say to ourselves—or think about ourselves—that determine the magnitude of our next steps.

The lies we tell ourselves are not from God, lies like: *I'm not smart enough or strong enough. I am stupid or too fat. Who is going to love me? I am not worthy. I will fail.* Why do we think such dreadful and wretched thoughts?

Why do we mutter words to ourselves that we would *never* say to another person? Why do we refuse to speak goodness into our own lives?

Today's lesson is about compassion, grace, and acceptance for our own selves. When we quiet our mind, we begin to hear the voices within. I am talking about self-talk. When your inner voice is talking, and it isn't saying anything good, that isn't from God. We need to take control of those inner voices and realize what is and is not from God. Tell your inner critic to be quiet and leave.

The motivation, encouragement, and words that tell us we are indeed good enough, strong enough, and pretty enough come from God. He gives us the understanding that while we are not perfect, we are still pretty fabulous. It is His voice we should be listening to.

Think about all of the experiences you've missed out on because of the lies you told yourself. No doubt there are many.

Remember this: We are all special. We have different gifts. The fire we have inside of us is unique to us. We cannot compare ourselves to others because those are the inner thoughts that ruin us.

We weren't made to be like everyone else, so why do we strive to be?

The next time your inner voice starts telling you that you aren't good enough—or you have any other self-sabotaging words—repeat this to yourself:

I am a child of God who is perfectly imperfect. I accept who I am, and I forgive myself for my past mistakes. I've learned from them, and I have become stronger. God didn't make me like anyone else. I am unique and beautiful. My head is held high and so are my standards.

Then give yourself a smile because you know those words are true.

I praise you because I am fearfully and wonderfully made;
your works are wonderful,
I know that full well.
Psalm 139:14

There are different kinds of gifts, but the same Spirit distributes them. There are different kinds of service, but the same Lord. There are different kinds of working, but in all of them and in everyone it is the same God at work. 1 Corinthians 12:4–6

Chapter 52

I Love You More

As we finish the section on overcoming, I want to end with some final thoughts on God's love.

Don't be afraid, for I am with you. Those words are awesome, aren't they? They mean you are never alone. Ever.

In the darkest of nights, God is there. In the intricate moments of our problems, God is there. He shows you that they aren't problems but things you need to go through.

When it seems like your soul cannot bear anymore, take heart, Jesus has overcome the world so that you can get through it with Him by your side.

When you think no one else could possibly understand what you are going though, Jesus can.

I know in your mind, you want to have it all figured out, but sometimes the answers don't come right away. It is okay. God designed it that way. You just have to trust him. He has a plan.

Take a deep breath and ponder His love for you. When I was young, my mom would stretch out her hands as far as she could and say, "I love you this much!" Well, God loves you the same way, except His arms reach out to infinity. Take that in.

Bring Him with you everywhere you go today, and you will notice your day become brighter and your burdens become lighter.

Anytime you are feeling frustrated or alone, happy or sad, troubled or at peace, know that God is with you.

"... and teaching them to obey everything I have commanded you. And surely I am with you always, to the very end of the age." Matthew 28:20

"Have I not commanded you? Be strong and courageous. Do not be afraid; do not be discouraged, for the LORD your God will be with you wherever you go." Joshua 1:9

You Can Find Joy in All Things

In every hardship you endure and overcome, know that you didn't do it alone. Acknowledge Him. Praise Him. We have the strength of the Holy Spirit within us. He gives us the ability to respond to any difficulty with His resources and His Word.

Take the things from the past that have controlled you and give them to God. Your past doesn't have to dictate your future. What do you need to let go of today?

Part 4

Things I Had to Learn the Hard Way

"What the Lord wants is that you shall go about the business to which He sets you, not asking for an easy post, nor grumbling at a hard one."

– Catherine Booth

Let's face it, ladies, our journey in business is much different than a man's, and that is okay. We have to work with what we've got. Here are some lessons I have learned along the way which have helped me become successful.

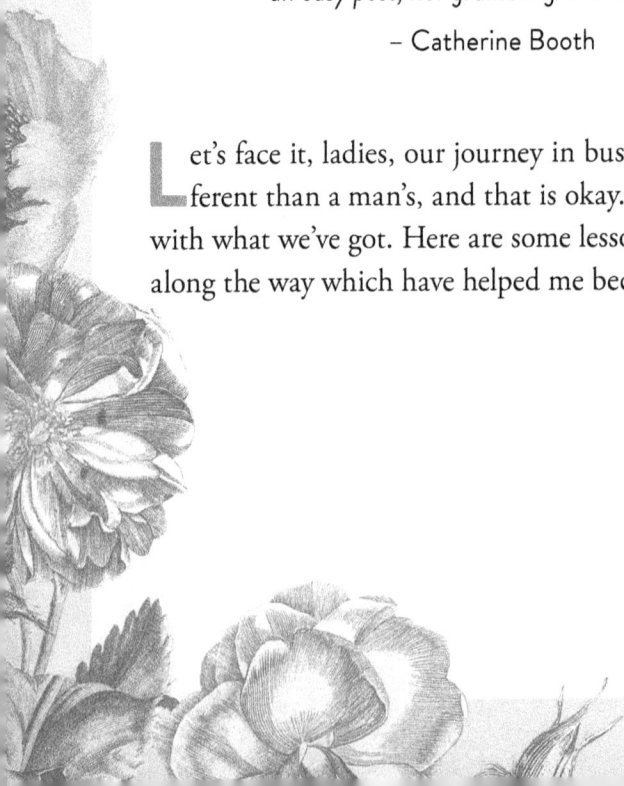

Chapter 53

What Is the Measure of Success?

The ultimate measure of success is not the amount money you make. It is not the amount of time you have to work. It is not the goals you crush. It rests in the answer to these two questions: Do you have a good relationship with God? Are you happy when you get home?

I just blew your mind a little bit, didn't I? It is not something we think naturally. Some of us imagine that having a job making lots of money and being able to buy whatever we want means we are successful. Perhaps we think success is working towards one goal after the next or being famous.

At the end of the day, is home where you want to be? Is it a place of peace and love? Are you excited to go home?

Do you spend time with God every day and work on your spirituality?

If your answer to those questions is no then I argue you are not truly successful. Unless your household is a place of happiness for you (and your family) and you spend time with God, then everything else you have done to make yourself successful has been for naught. We need balance.

Without the unity of work, family/home life, and spirituality, you won't be successful. I am talking about *real* success here. The union is the cornerstone of contentedness, yet so many people forget to build their empires with these important materials. It isn't easy because it takes a different kind of grit and gumption. Many won't put in the additional effort and set their eyes on material success instead of wholehearted success.

It is not money, fame, accolades, or power that make you successful in life. If you set your mind on those things, you won't ever be happy.

When you work hard towards your career goals, familial relationships, and God that is what really matters. When you have equilibrium, you have success. You won't give a care if you are rich or famous because you will realize what you do have moves far beyond that.

He has shown you, O mortal, what is good.
And what does the Lord require of you?
To act justly and to love mercy
and to walk humbly with your God. Micah 6:8
Whoever loves money never has enough;
whoever loves wealth is never satisfied with their income.
This too is meaningless. Ecclesiastes 5:10
Unless the Lord builds the house,
the builders labor in vain.
Unless the Lord watches over the city,
the guards stand watch in vain.
In vain you rise early
and stay up late,
toiling for food to eat—
for he grants sleep to those he loves.
Psalm 127:1–2

Do not wear yourself out to get rich;
do not trust your own cleverness.
Proverbs 23:4

Chapter 54

Don't Stress Yourself or Else You Will Wreck Yourself

A thought has been on my mind recently. It has to do with stress.

We say, "I have a high threshold for stress" like it is a badge of honor. Why is that a good thing, anyway?

Why do we pat ourselves on the back and boast about having a high stress tolerance? Shouldn't it be a bad thing? What ever happened to balance?

Stress is a state of mental or emotional strain or tension resulting from adverse or demanding circumstances. It is supposed to be a temporary state, not one that lasts a lifetime. It is designed to make us pay attention to what is going on and make us more driven to make things happen for a short period of time.

In our society, *not* having a high threshold for stress is seen as a sign of weakness.

Having consistently high stress levels is a bad thing, a very bad thing. It not only affects your health but also those around you. We should not celebrate high stress levels. We should appreciate and commend those with true balance, those who have figured out that the more stress tolerance you have, the more stress you have. Congratulations!

We have to recognize that a constant level of stress in our lives only breeds dysfunction, less empathy, constant pressure, and makes us operate well-below our true potential. Think about when your stress is high. Do you think clearly? Do you worry about the pressure you are under to get things done? Are you living life in a chaotic frenzy? When we allow ourselves to take on high stress levels all the time, everyone suffers. We become gluttons for punishment because we believe we can take everything on with no consideration of our limitations or need for rest.

What can be done? We need to *lower* our tolerance for stress and learn to say no. Don't take so much on. Know your limitations.

Have enough self-awareness to pay attention to when you feel stress. If you start to feel it, it is because you are quickly approaching your limitations. Take a quick break. Stop accepting so many things into your never-ending pile of things to do. Learn to delegate and ask for help if you need it.

Set proper expectations with others as to what you can and cannot do, as well as what you are willing to do or not do. Draw boundaries.

Meditate. Pray. Journal. Work out. Pay attention to yourself! There needs to be a balance.

I don't know about you, but I am done living my life in a frenzy. It is not worth it. The constant high levels of stress I put upon myself took a toll on me and those I love. It was always, "Yes! Yes! Yes!" and "More! More! More!"

Now I say, "No, thank you." I have really taken my life back. Living life in a constant state of feverishness was insanity.

So today I leave you with my thoughts on stress. We all need to reevaluate ourselves and stop accepting high stress level management as a trophy.

Lower your tolerance to stress and you will have less stress. It is that simple!

Cast your burden on the LORD, and He shall sustain you; He shall never permit the righteous to be moved. Psalm 55:22 NKJV

Now may the Lord of peace himself give you peace at all times and in every way. The Lord be with all of you. 2 Thessalonians 3:16

Lord, you alone are my portion and my cup;
you make my lot secure.
The boundary lines have fallen for me in pleasant places;
surely, I have a delightful inheritance.
I will praise the LORD, who counsels me;
even at night my heart instructs me.
I keep my eyes always on the LORD.
With him at my right hand, I will not be shaken.
Therefore my heart is glad and my tongue rejoices;
my body also will rest secure.
Psalm 16:5–9

Chapter 55

Just a Small-Town Girl, Working in a Man's World— How to Survive in a Male- Dominated Industry

The next several chapters are going to cover some of the dynamics of being a boss babe, a Christian, and a respectable leader.

Working in a mainly male dominated industry—and succeeding greatly within it—carries an interesting dynamic. I am going to do my best to explain to you how it feels, how to do it, and how I have found to act within it. I am going to put the reality of the good, the bad, and the ugly all out there for you.

First, I have to say some of my core beliefs when it comes to women and men in the workplace. I do believe that there are jobs men should mostly do and vice versa. Military combat and other highly physical things which require a lot of strength, for the most part, I would consider a man's job. I don't believe women should play with men on the NFL field. Men are just better suited for it. That is the reality.

Anything or any career that involves your brain is fair play and for anyone, man or woman. It is a simple as that. I also don't consider myself a feminist. So that is not what this is all about. I am also not here to make women mad because they feel a woman can do any job a man can. In a way that is true, but please realize there are certain things men in general are simply better at—and other things women in general are simply better at. That is all I am saying.

So if you are a woman who finds herself in an industry (such as mine) where the males way outweigh the females and you want to know the best way to excel, read on.

The bottom line is you are going to have to work harder in the beginning to prove yourself so that others take you seriously. Then after that, you will likely have to continuously prove yourself in one way or the other. Yeah, I know. It is not fair. Then again, who ever said life was fair? No one.

You chose to work in a male-dominated field though, so you knew what you were getting into. It is okay though, because staying on your toes only makes you better and stronger. It doesn't allow you to become complacent or lazy because either you won't survive or you will fail miserably. The mere fact that you have to work harder is only going to help you be so much better than you would have been without the competition.

There are so many complex components we deal with, I know. Let's take a look at some things to think about over the next few chapters.

THE QUANDARY OF BEING STRONG AND ASSERTIVE WITHOUT BEING A TOTAL WENCH.

This is an age-old problem that requires a balancing act. I know, it is a double standard, but there is nothing you can do about it other than showing others that one way of acting does not equate to the another way of being perceived (even though some people will still think you are a wench, and that is okay because you cannot please everyone).

Being strong doesn't mean you must be conniving, take short cuts, undermine others, walk all over people, or treat others horribly. If you do those things, then you are a total jerk regardless of what sex you are.

Being strong in the workplace is about knowing who you are, knowing your stuff, and not being afraid to let other people know that. It means speaking up. It means being involved. It means doing what you say you are going to do. It means stepping up, knowing the rules better than anyone else, and knowing how to talk to people. Present your ideas without being afraid. Don't give up. Don't back down or hide in a corner when something goes wrong. These are the things that make you strong. You don't have to be a shrew if you are a strong woman. You just have to be capable, competent, and qualified—maybe a little more so than the guy next to you.

You are going to get left out, dismissed, and ignored. If you want to survive and thrive though, you will have to brush yourself off and keep going. They will take notice. Just keep being yourself. Work hard. Learn. Grow. You *must* have confidence in yourself and your abilities.

If anyone speaks, they should do so as one who speaks the very words of God. If anyone serves, they should do so with the strength God provides, so that in all things God may be praised through Jesus Christ. To him be the glory and the power for ever and ever. Amen. 1 Peter 4:11

Wisdom reposes in the heart of the discerning and even among fools she lets herself be known. Proverbs 14:33

Chapter 56

The Handshake—How to Do It Right!

Whatever you do in life, make sure you learn the proper way to shake another person's hand. We are not in the year 1850. It is time to shake a hand like you mean it.

Don't be a dead fish. Don't put your hand out like someone is going to kiss it.

A good handshake is serious business. It shows you are serious. It shows that you are strong. It shows that you are confident. A weak or plain silly handshake shows you are weak and don't know how to conduct yourself in a business setting.

You are welcome!

The wise woman builds her house,
but with her own hands the foolish one tears hers down.
Proverbs 14:1

Chapter 57

Dealing with Other Women and Men at Work

DEALING WITH WOMEN AT WORK

If you find yourself in a higher or more successful position in the company than most other women, there is going be some drama and some jealousy. You are going to be looked at in a different way. The other women are going to watch you closely, whether for the sake of being envious, proud, or jealous. You are going to be talked about. It's okay. Why women do this in general has always been one of life's biggest mysteries, but women do it all the time.

We compare. Whenever another woman walks into a room and we perceive her as better (better looking, richer, or more successful) than us, we immediately compare ourselves to that person even though we have no base knowledge of anything other than what we imagine in our heads. Women need to stop doing that anyway. It will make our lives so much better.

So here's the thing. I believe it is so important to be kind to everyone. From the lady who cleans your office, to the head of the company, be kind. Obviously, this goes for everyone and every aspect of life. If we all practiced a little kindness and acknowledged people more, this world would be a better place. Don't be fake though because people can see right through it when you are. Being phony is only going to hurt you. Treat people with respect regardless of their position and genuinely love them. It will make a difference.

When you become successful, it can be easy to forget the so-called little people because you are so laser-focused on success. It can also be easy to think you have something to prove and thus treat others poorly. Don't do that. Be kind. Acknowledge others. Smile.

Now, I am not saying that by doing this, there isn't going to be drama, jealousy, and judgment where you work. Some people just aren't going to like you. Remember though that 99.99999% of the time, it is not about you. Many simply have something going on inside them that has nothing to do with you. My advice: Ignore the behavior. If it becomes an issue, confront it directly with the person and talk it out until it becomes a non-issue. You would be surprised at how quickly rumors and nonsense stop once the source is confronted. People are going to talk, and there will be haters. It is okay.

Bottom line: Be the same self you were before you became successful.

You should also align yourself with other powerful women in your field. I am not necessarily talking about women who are at your level in pay. I just mean strong women you can build up and have as confidants and encouragers.

DEALING WITH MEN AT WORK

This is where it gets interesting because there are so many factors I need to talk about.

I will start with how a woman should dress, especially when intwined in a male-dominated field. Women . . . please don't dress like a harlot. Yes, I said that. You are only inviting trouble. The easiest way for someone *not* to take you seriously is for you to dress provocatively in the workplace. If you are wearing an outfit you have also worn out to clubs, then it is not what you should be wearing to work.

A woman's sexual "power" should not be used at work if you want people to respect you. It is true. Most men are distracted by shiny things, and you don't want anyone to only look at you sexually because of the distracting and inappropriate outfit you are wearing. You want them to pay attention to you because of how smart you are—not because they want to have sex with you.

It doesn't take money to be classy. Be modest. This is not me telling you to dress like a nun, just be classy. It is more powerful.

Secondly, you will likely have to deal with men hitting on you. It is just the dynamic of a hundred guys for every five women. It is a fine line we have to walk, I know. You don't want to be one of those people who won't engage with others, but you also don't want to be the office flirt who uses her sexuality to get favors and the mirage of more business because of that. You just have to be careful.

When you have a problem at home, don't use the men at work as your confidants. Doing so is dangerous. When you go out for happy hour with the crew, don't get drunk and stay out too late. Be respectful of yourself and others will follow suit. Remember, you want others to respect you for your hard work and contributions, not think of you as the woman who can't hold her stuff together at a bar.

If someone hits on you or asks you out, I would advise not going out with them, but if you do, make sure you keep your workspace professional and don't bring your romance into the office. It makes people uncomfortable, and it is the quickest way for people to make judgments—whether right or wrong. It will quickly knock down the progress you have worked so hard to build for yourself.

If you don't want to go out with the person, let them know you are flattered, but not interested. You don't date people from work. Then drop it. Be cordial and not weird about it.

Attraction is a natural dynamic in life between men and women together. Don't be offended if someone asks you out.

However, there is a huge difference between the above and true sexual harassment. Someone who makes you feel uncomfortable, any creepy leering, inappropriate touching, or unwanted and unrelenting advances are harassment. I am sad to say that I have been a victim of this many times over the past twenty years, and it is something a lot of women have to deal with on a daily basis. It sucks. We can make everyone watch every sexual harassment video in the world, but this is going to happen unfortunately. Even more in a field dominated by men with you being one of the few women around.

So what can you do? When I was young, I just took it, for lack of better words. I used to ignore it even though it made me feel uncomfortable. I refused to engage. I didn't tell anyone about it either. No one prepared me for this!

Now, my honest, personal answer (which may not be the totally correct answer) is that I confront the person who is doing it away from others. I pull them aside at what I perceive is the right time, and I demand for them to stop. I let them know firmly that if they do not stop, I will let HR know about their actions. I take a very straightforward, no-nonsense approach. I let them know what they are doing and how it makes me feel. So far, I have not had to report anyone because the inappropriate behavior stopped immediately after my confrontation.

The right answer might be to follow whatever your company's policy is regarding sexual harassment in the workplace. I don't do that, but it is my decision to take care of things on my own. So far it has worked out for me. Maybe one day it won't, but I will deal with that when if happens.

You also have to be careful not to put yourself into situations where things could happen. Don't linger at happy hours or stay out late. That is when things tend to happen. It's not a lovely thing to say, but it is a true thing to say.

What I don't recommend is being dramatic in the office in a way that lets everyone know that so-and-so is a total creeper and makes you feel uncomfortable. Behavior like that tends to backfire. When you are surrounded by mostly guys, making a huge deal out of things doesn't work in your favor. Be discreet because not doing so takes away from who you are as a leader in your industry or field.

In our world of political correctness, there are also some women who take things a little too sensitively. When you are in a male-dominated industry (or anywhere in life actually), learning to take some things (I am talking things not meant to be malicious) with a grain of salt will help you profusely. People want to be able to joke without feeling the need to walk on eggshells around you because they know you might get offended by the slightest thing. You are going to isolate yourself from everyone if you are that person.

"Watch and pray so that you will not fall into temptation. The spirit is willing, but the flesh is weak." Matthew 26:41

But the fruit of the Spirit is love, joy, peace, forbearance, kindness, goodness, faithfulness, gentleness and self-control. Against such things there is no law. Galatians 5:22–23

Chapter 58

Fitting in—Being "One of the Guys"

This is the fun part. How do we, as women, fit in to the male-dominated industry we are in while maintaining the respect we have earned, showing we know our stuff, and continuing to be taken seriously for what we know? It is a tough mix to juggle, but it is only the reality of what we need to do.

When you work with a bunch of dudes, being a part of the team is important, which means that you will have to be one of the guys sometimes. It is by virtue of your circumstance and career choice. I don't think it is wise to isolate yourself from everyone.

You don't want to be the outsider. You want them to feel comfortable in front of you while at the same time, not so comfortable that they stop treating you with respect. Like I said earlier, if you have casted yourself to be the one that everyone has to walk on eggshells with, then being part of the team isn't going to be real. It will be only superficial.

People need to feel comfortable around you. When they do, they will want to include you. You want to be yourself as if you were around brothers. It seems so silly and simple, but it is true!

It is important though, that when someone crosses the line, you deal with it swiftly and strongly so it doesn't happen again.

Don't be the one who brings drama into the office or cries if someone makes you mad. Doing things like that will only serve to bring down your credibility.

Finally, don't be afraid to speak up. Share your ideas. Provide feedback. Don't just focus on the fact that you are a minority in your environment. Don't expect special treatment on a daily basis because you are a woman. Work your tail off and show them who you are on the inside.

You may have chosen a male-dominated field, so you are going to have to use your IQ and EQ in order to succeed in such an environment. Be strong. Be courageous. Don't back down. We have a lot more work to do in these instances than other women in different fields. We can do it.

One more thing. What I am not saying here is that you have to change who you are in order to work in a male-dominated industry or workplace. You may have to modify some of your behaviors.

Let us not become weary in doing good, for at the proper time we will reap a harvest if we do not give up. Galatians 6:9

You will eat the fruit of your labor;
blessings and prosperity will be yours.
Psalm 128:2

So whether you eat or drink or whatever you do, do it all for the glory of God. 1 Corinthians 10:31

Chapter 59

I Don't Want to Be a Dude: The Quandary of Being the Boss at Work and a Lady at Home

S peaking of dudes. I don't know about you, but I want to be a lady. I know I am not the only woman who struggles with this paradox.

How can an alpha woman balance both her masculine side and her feminine side? How can we embrace both sides of us so that one doesn't overtake the other?

My personality is of greater yang. Every personality test puts me as a Commander. I am an ENTJ-A. I am an extrovert, intuitive woman who thinks more than I feel sometimes. My levels of assertiveness are off the charts, and I will find a way to make something happen or make my own way. I am self-programmed to be tough, no-nonsense, and straight-forward. The hustle is natural to me, and I thrive on it. It has made me wildly successful in business. I flourish on solving problems, taking charge, leading, having big dreams and goals, and keeping my eye on future goals. I get stuff done. I have no problem juggling a hundred things at a time, and I don't need help with anything. I am basically a man in a skirt at times.

I just talked about how women have to be strong working in a man's world if we want to be successful. We have to be dude-like if we want to do well. That is true. We have to be assertive and draw clear boundaries. It is just the way it is, and I am perfectly okay with it—at work.

However, in the personal side of my life, I don't want to be a dude. Every strong, successful woman I know feels the exact same way. While we are like men at work, we do *not* want to be like men at home, and this is where the struggle is real.

I want to be taken care of—for lack of better words—at home. I want security and comfort. I want to know everything is going to be okay. I want to turn off work-Jen and turn on the Jen that is feminine and soft. It is harder to do than you would think. Over the years, I have been working on this. Lately, I have felt myself wanting to shift my balance to the more feminine side of myself and embrace it. I want the man to be the man and myself to be the woman in the relationship in an old-school biblical sense.

How do strong women flip that switch? It is not easy. We have to let go. Whether we like it or not, two masculine sides in a relationship don't work well and never will. In order to have balance, someone has to be masculine and the other feminine. Your man wants to be with a woman, not a clone of himself.

Over the years, we have been taught so much about feminism and it has changed some things for the better, but I truly believe there is a dirty side to all of that. I believe feminism is also toxic when it comes to relationships. I don't know about you, but I don't want to be like my guy. I want to be treated like a woman. Ladies, there is nothing better than being with a man who is the true spiritual leader of your home, a man who opens your doors, cares for you, provides for you, and stands up for you—a man who is a man.

We have to realize that we do not have to do *everything* on our own. We don't have to struggle alone. We do not have to constantly prove ourselves to our partners, we can receive. We need to accept that there is someone willing to take care of us emotionally and provide the comfort and security our souls crave so very much. We don't have to always be the leaders and commanders.

Accept help. Listen more. Be playful. Let your man be the man. We need to have roles in our families. We don't have to push so hard, stress so hard, or prove a damn thing to anyone.

Valuing and embracing the beauty we have both within and outside of us doesn't make us a shallow person. We need to enhance our natural beauty and appreciate our true nature.

We need to connect to our feminine energy. It is that wild energy flowing within that so many have stomped so far down it's hard to see its light any more. We have to stop going against our feminine nature.

What makes you feel the most beautiful and sexy? Do more of that.

What do you like to create? Create more.

Spend time in silence, prayer, and meditation.

Spend less time on social media and watching the news.

Give yourself permission to relax and just be.

Accentuate the positives in your physical beauty.

Study femininity and what it means to be feminine.

Let the man lead.

A wife of noble character who can find?
She is worth far more than rubies.
Her husband has full confidence in her
and lacks nothing of value.
She brings him good, not harm,
all the days of her life.

She selects wool and flax
and works with eager hands.
She is like the merchant ships,
bringing her food from afar.
She gets up while it is still night;
she provides food for her family
and portions for her female servants.
She considers a field and buys it;
out of her earnings she plants a vineyard.
She sets about her work vigorously;
her arms are strong for her tasks.
She sees that her trading is profitable,
and her lamp does not go out at night.
In her hand she holds the distaff
and grasps the spindle with her fingers.
She opens her arms to the poor
and extends her hands to the needy.
When it snows, she has no fear for her household;
for all of them are clothed in scarlet.
She makes coverings for her bed;
she is clothed in fine linen and purple.
Her husband is respected at the city gate,
where he takes his seat among the elders of the land.
She makes linen garments and sells them,
and supplies the merchants with sashes.
She is clothed with strength and dignity;
she can laugh at the days to come.
She speaks with wisdom,
and faithful instruction is on her tongue.
She watches over the affairs of her household
and does not eat the bread of idleness.
Her children arise and call her blessed;
her husband also, and he praises her:
"Many women do noble things,

but you surpass them all."
Charm is deceptive, and beauty is fleeting;
but a woman who fears the LORD *is to be praised.*
Honor her for all that her hands have done,
and let her works bring her praise at the city gate.
Proverbs 31:10–31

Submit to one another out of reverence for Christ. Wives, submit your-
selves to your own husbands as you do to the Lord. For the husband is the
head of the wife as Christ is the head of the church, his body, of which he
is the Savior. Now as the church submits to Christ, so also wives should
submit to their husbands in everything.

Husbands, love your wives, just as Christ loved the church and gave him-
self up for her to make her holy, cleansing her by the washing with water
through the word, and to present her to himself as a radiant church, with-
out stain or wrinkle or any other blemish, but holy and blameless. In this
same way, husbands ought to love their wives as their own bodies. He who
loves his wife loves himself. Ephesians 5:21–28

Me! I learned how to flip that switch.

Chapter 60

Morning Routines

Morning routines have improved my life immeasurably. Sure, getting up at 4:30 every morning (except on the weekends, unless my body magically wakes up at that time) is tough sometimes. It would be so much easier to lay in bed all nice and warm, but I get up anyway and I don't ever regret it.

It is like working out. There has never been a workout I have regretted after actually doing it. It is the getting there part I struggle with sometimes.

My morning routine consists of us rising together and the hubs making me a cup of amazing coffee. We sit in our chairs, and we have all of our books and journals next to us on the table, so they are easy to access. When I was single, I made my own coffee and sat by myself.

Then we sit and think, read, pray, journal. We think of the specific things we are grateful for. We do this for an hour.

Then I work out for an hour-ish before I taking my shower and getting ready for the day. I don't get to work until nine.

So before I even go to work, I have been up and productive for almost five hours.

I want to focus on that first hour of the morning, the time for prayer and meditation and what that does for me.

Spending time with God as part of my morning routine is the best hour of my day. It is the most important. It is the most powerful.

Spending time to be grateful, to think about how God is working in my life, and meditating on His Word about whatever is on my heart that morning is the most paramount part of the day.

My mind is cleared and my heart opens. With my thoughts unscrambled, I am ready to hear what God has to say to me.

Thinking of specific things I am grateful for has made me even more grateful for the beautiful life I lead. It is really cool how that works: The more grateful you are, the more you realize just how many things you have to be grateful for.

Sometimes I love what He puts on my heart. Sometimes He tells me something I don't necessarily want to hear, a change I need to make, or something that I should do. I pray for people, I pray to be a light in the world, I pray for direction, and I pray for God to show me the true hearts of the people in my life. Sometimes I don't love what He reveals, and that is okay. I have learned that when a door shuts, there is something so much better in store.

Spending this precious hour clears the day ahead of me. It removes obstacles I thought I had and helps put me on a straight path. The path might not necessarily be the one I had intended, but that really doesn't matter. I learned long ago that in the end, it is not up to me at all. So now I just go with it.

He gives me insights and glimpses of the life He wants me to lead.

I listen.

This is something I have struggled with in the past—the actual listening part. Even when I hear Him loud and clear, sometimes I don't truly listen, and then I don't take action either. I want to go my own way and on my own path because I know what I am doing. We know how that all turns out. I have definitely gotten so much better at the taking action part also. Even when I don't want to, I know His way is so much better.

My day starts peacefully and without all of the frazzle and rushing around. It is beautiful, and I hope I will continue to do it throughout all of the days of my life.

It is so much better than waking up at the last second and rushing to get ready for work. You should try it!

Your word is a lamp for my feet,
a light on my path.
Psalm 119:105

But seek first his kingdom and his righteousness, and all these things will
be given to you as well. Matthew 6:33

Listen to advice and accept discipline,
and at the end you will be counted among the wise.
Proverbs 19:20

Let the message of Christ dwell among you richly as you teach and admon-
ish one another with all wisdom through psalms, hymns, and songs from
the Spirit, singing to God with gratitude in your hearts. Colossians 3:16

Our daily morning routine.

Chapter 61

Work Ethic Eliminates
Fear . . . Don't You Know?

When I was young, we really didn't have a whole lot compared with kids now-a-days. My brother and I grew up in a middle-class family in Buffalo, NY. My dad was a cop and my mom had her own photography business. We had a comfortable home.

My mom taught my brother and I to be very self-sufficient. We had to. Nothing was really given to us so we worked for it.

At eleven years old, I got a paper route. Back in the 80s, kids mostly delivered newspapers. I had my own wagon for the Sunday papers because they were so full of ads, and then I had my trusty paper bag for the other days. Every day after school, I lugged the heavy newspapers up and down one and one-half streets and on the weekends I did it early in the morning—rain or snow.

Newspapers had to be delivered or I would be in trouble. I had to put each paper at the front or the side door depending on what each client wanted. I wonder sometimes how I retained that information for the eighty to one hundred houses I delivered to, but somehow I did. Then each week, I had to collect the payment of the newspapers—not fun. Imagine a young kid knocking on your door asking for payment for the weekly newspaper delivery. I laugh thinking about it now. I had to grow courage to do the job because it was quite intimidating, and I quickly learned that there are a lot of strange people in this world!

When Christmastime came around, it was all worth it. I would rake in massive tips. The other eleven months of thankless work became totally doable because during the month of December, I would get around $300 bucks in tips. That was a lot of money for a kid in the 80s. I felt rich! Ha!

Fast forward a few years, I began working at the age of fifteen at a supermarket as a cashier. I would walk there on the way home from High School. Notice I said walk. We walked about two miles a day each way to school, whether rain, snow, or sun. (No, I wasn't barefoot, and it wasn't uphill.) I would work for 3 hours or whatever was allowed by law and then either get picked up or walk home.

We didn't have fancy clothes because we could never afford them but I really didn't care about that back then. I didn't know what those things were. We didn't have any fancy stuff. All was good in the world. Somehow, I survived.

One of my parents, I forget who, co-signed on a loan with me for $1,200 so I could buy my first car. It was a sexy light green Oldsmobile Supreme. Oh, how I loved that car. I paid it back out of the money I earned from work, about $100 per month for twelve months. The car was mine.

I used to compare myself with others and what they got and honestly, back then, I would get a little jealous when my friends' parents bought them a car or took them on fancy ski vacations.

Now, I am so very thankful to my parents for not spoiling me. I learned valuable lessons. If you want something, well, work for it.

Many people have asked me what the secret is to my success.

When I work, I work. I am laser-focused, and I don't put stuff off. I get the job done right the first time, which my Dad did teach me.

When things are given to you, entitlement happens. Spoiled kids become lazy adults. It is a disservice people do to their kids when they give them everything.

Why are so many people afraid to work hard now-a-days?

Working hard is the only way to be successful. Success is not given, it is *earned*. You don't deserve to be successful. You are only successful if you work at it every day.

Can I get an amen?

All hard work brings a profit,
but mere talk leads only to poverty.
Proverbs 14:23

We work hard with our own hands. When we are cursed, we bless; when we are persecuted, we endure it. 1 Corinthians 4:12

"For all those who exalt themselves will be humbled, and those who humble themselves will be exalted." Luke 14:11

Chapter 62

Working 24/7

Recently, I saw a post on Facebook from a person looking for a referral for a business open after normal work hours. They weren't satisfied with the company they were currently using because it wasn't open at night "when the clients were available." So they were looking for someone else to help. Below that post was a whole bunch of professionals chiming in about how they are always available, 24/7.

I began to wonder why we brag about being available 24/7. That is not something to brag about. Why do we continue to make this our standard? What is wrong?

It is insane. Congratulations for not protecting every evening, holiday, weekend, and vacation and for giving your family the message that they are not important enough for you to be present.

Now, I know some of you are thinking, *Jen, you are wrong. A career in (insert profession here) has allowed me a lot of freedom.* I am not saying it doesn't. But is it truly freedom if you stop whatever you are doing to pick up the phone or answer an email? Maybe we need to redefine what freedom truly is.

We have become servants to work, simply because we have allowed it and welcomed it. We brag to others about our constant availability.

Which clients most often waste the most of your time? I bet it is the ones who call and text at all hours of the day and night. I bet it is the ones who expect you to drop whatever you are doing to help them even though you told them you have something else going on.

Who are your best clients? I bet it is the ones who respect your time.

Everyone should create a few boundaries. They will change your life. Pick eight hours a day and work. Give your clients and job your full attention, and let them know ahead of time when you work and how you work. You'd be surprised at what setting proper expectations ahead of time does.

I also understand that, on occasion, you absolutely will have to let a client know something after normal hours or stay that extra time to get something done. I am not talking about that type of situation here.

I am talking about stopping your whole life whenever the phone rings. I am talking about if it doesn't matter the holiday, the vacation, the time of day, or who you are with, you pick up the phone. I am talking about how much time you give to your job or client late in the evenings or while you are supposed to be spending time with your family.

Stop bragging about being available 24/7. It is not something to boast about. It is out of control and the last thing we should be perpetuating is that our time and our life doesn't matter.

We need to have the tough conversations about how this standard messes up our relationships. Enough is enough. Put down the phone and stop using the computer. Whatever it is likely won't matter five years from now.

Being present does. All of the money in the world won't bring back time. Please enjoy it.

I have a sign in my office that says, "Don't ever get so busy making a living that you forget to make a life."

Don't be afraid to stand up and stand alone in a world where people will think you are crazy. Take comfort in knowing one of the world's greatest secrets—they are the crazy ones.

Do not wear yourself out to get rich;
do not trust your own cleverness.
Cast but a glance at riches, and they are gone,
for they will surely sprout wings
and fly off to the sky like an eagle.
Proverbs 23:4–5

Then he said to them, "Watch out! Be on your guard against all kinds of greed; life does not consist in an abundance of possessions." Luke 12:15

Return to your rest, my soul,
for the Lord has been good to you.
Psalm 116:7

A balanced life is the key to success. On top
of submarine rock, praising God.

Chapter 63

"God has No Business in Business"

God has no business in business. You really need to separate the two.

That is what some have told me as I have become more and more vocal about where He lies in my success. I just sit there and smile. I think to myself, and most times say, "God *is* the reason I am where I am today."

You see, I will unashamedly give Him the glory for my success. With Him, I have been able to accomplish amazing things. What better partner in business is there than the Ultimate Collaborator, the Most High Teammate, and the Most Amazing Confidant?

Exactly.

Imagine a world where no one was afraid to bring God into everything that they did, a world where we didn't have to feel ashamed or afraid to share the light that wants so badly to beam out of us.

Take off that ridiculous cloak you feel like you have to wear in order to not offend others. Be proud of your Christianity and give God the glory and thanksgiving for the millions of blessings before you each day. Some will love you for it. Others will hate you. It won't matter though because the only opinion that really matters is His, and you know how He will feel about all of that.

I am not saying to force others to believe what you believe. No one can successfully do that. It doesn't work. However, when someone sees the light within you, share it.

That is what we are supposed to do.

Every good and perfect gift is from above, coming down from the Father of the heavenly lights, who does not change like shifting shadows. James 1:17

What good is it for someone to gain the whole world, yet forfeit their soul? Mark 8:36

Therefore go and make disciples of all nations, baptizing them in the name of the Father and of the Son and of the Holy Spirit, and teaching them to obey everything I have commanded you. And surely I am with you always, to the very end of the age." Matthew 28:19–20

CBC bookstore holding my first book, *The Storm*.

Chapter 64

Intimidation Factor

Many of us have an intimidation factor with various people in our lives who we hold in higher regard than ourselves.

I remember when I first started out in business, I would get intimidated when I talked to someone I regarded as more affluent and successful than I was. I held them in such high regard.

As the years have passed, I can tell you that I have learned one thing: we are all just people! No matter what someone does or how much success they have had or currently have, they are still just a human being. They wake up, go to the bathroom, eat, put clothes on, and have good and bad days. No one person is much different than anyone else. A job is a job, and it definitely does not make you who you are.

So I started looking at people differently. Instead of looking at what they did, I looked at who they were as people. I looked at what their hearts were like. Success, I learned, was something that could be attained by anyone.

When I stopped being afraid of people and feeling bad about myself in the presence of someone else, I found the confidence to conquer my goals. If this person, who was just another person, could do it, so could I.

When you start looking at people differently, you see that everyone deserves your respect.

Instead of being intimidated, be inspired.

I can do all this through him who gives me strength. Philippians 4:13

Chapter 65

Show Some Class, Will Ya?
Your Clothes Do Some Talkin'

O h, Facebook, how I love-hate you. As I scrolled through recently, I saw picture after picture of women putting it all out there—who also, in the same feed, try to portray themselves as professionals. When did this become okay? Where has class gone?

I get it, sex sells. When we post pictures as described above, what exactly are we selling anyway? Do we want someone to do business with us because of our cleavage or because we are great at what we do?

As women, when we dress this way and act this way, it takes away the legitimacy of whatever profession we are in. Many people may not like that statement, but it is true.

People confuse attractiveness with sexiness. They are not the same. We may think that less will bring us more, but in reality, the only thing we are getting more of is people shaking their heads at our hypocrisy. It is unrealistic to show off so blatantly and then in the same sentence expect people to take you seriously. It doesn't work that way.

Our overall appearance, confidence, and mannerisms give impressions to others. We are a walking brand of ourselves, and there is only one opportunity to give a great first impression. Remember that.

Elegance and class are the qualities we should emulate.

She is clothed with strength and dignity;
she can laugh at the days to come.
She speaks with wisdom,
and faithful instruction is on her tongue. Proverbs 31:25–26

We are a walking brand of ourselves, and there is only
one opportunity to give a great first impression.

Chapter 66

The Art of Saying No

Saying no is empowering, and it is a skill I have focused on recently with great results.

"No" sets boundaries. It allows me to finally enjoy so many more things because I am not running around doing 54,000 other things that I don't want to do—all because I said no.

So many of us—especially women—feel guilty when asked to do something so we automatically say yes when asked, knowing full well we don't have the time to do it. We are so tired and so over-scheduled up because of this. We end up regretting saying yes more times than not and then we don't enjoy doing what we have committed to, ending up with resentment and disdain toward the task.

I am here to tell you that everyone needs to learn the art of saying no. It is way easier than you think.

When someone asks you to do something, don't answer right away. Let them know you will look at your schedule. Take time to decide if it is something you *really* want to do—and have the time to do. Then if it is, do it. Otherwise, politely decline.

Now, declining is the hard part because it makes us very uncomfortable. We are potentially hurting someone's feelings and people pleasers find that so hard to do. We don't want someone else mad at us. It will not be the end of the world, I promise. People will respect you for it.

Trust me, I am not saying I have become an expert at this fine art, but I am getting there. I have started saying no more and more often and it feels good. I no longer go places or do things I truly don't want to do (unless a good friend or family *really* needs me) only to hate every second. Time is the most precious commodity and one we cannot get back or get more of. I work hard during the week, and my time after work has become mine to spend as I please.

I started doing this a few years ago. Everyone at work thought I was nuts. I decided not to take calls after 5:30pm and to not work on the weekends. A real estate professional who doesn't work 24-7 . . . yup, that is me. Guess what? It has not hurt my business one bit.

Any person who does not respect your time in the beginning of the process will continue to not respect your time. Back in the days when I would pick up my phone late at night or on a Sunday, I very quickly realized that these people were unprepared time wasters. Gone are the days of me taking loan apps for someone who knew they were going to go house shopping for weeks but didn't take the twenty minutes prior to the weekend to get pre-qualified. I have learned that it is okay to say no. My personal time is extremely important.

So when you are tempted to feel guilty about saying no, I urge you to *pause*. Think about how hard you have worked this week and all the five million other things you need to take care of or that you would rather do. Politely say no if it is too much.

Above all, my brothers and sisters, do not swear—not by heaven or by earth or by anything else. All you need to say is a simple "Yes" or "No." Otherwise you will be condemned. James 5:12

Let your conversation be always full of grace, seasoned with salt, so that you may know how to answer everyone. Colossians 4:6

Chapter 67

Hold on Loosely

W hen I was younger, I was all about titles—youngest this, top that, best at that. Everything in my life revolved around my titles. My ambition and ego got the best of me, and I railroaded anyone who got in my way. I was a real jerk.

We let things like titles, power, jobs, and material things define us. We shouldn't, but we do anyway. We try and hold onto them so tightly at times, and we become absolutely devastated when they go away. We don't get it. We don't understand that these things should not be what defines our lives, yet they do.

We need to be prepared to see them all go away. Instead of clinging to them tightly, we need to loosen our grip and be prepared to let go.

What a spectacular waste of energy it is to hold on tightly to earthly treasures because of the fear of what will happen if they went away. Doing so lets them define you, and what we don't realize is that all they really are is a bunch of cacophonic noise that distracts us from concentrating on the stuff that really matters. So hold on loosely.

There is so much freedom in the realization that you are much more precious than the superficial things you have held in such high regard.

The *only* thing you should hold tightly to is God's hand. The other stuff doesn't matter.

Your job doesn't define you. Your wealth doesn't define you. If you lost all of those things tomorrow, you would still be who you are. Remember that.

"When someone invites you to a wedding feast, do not take the place of honor, for a person more distinguished than you may have been invited. If so, the host who invited both of you will come and say to you, 'Give this person your seat.' Then, humiliated, you will have to take the least important place. But when you are invited, take the lowest place, so that when your host comes, he will say to you, 'Friend, move up to a better place.' Then you will be honored in the presence of all the other guests. For all those who exalt themselves will be humbled, and those who humble themselves will be exalted." Luke 14:8–11

When pride comes, then comes disgrace,
but with humility comes wisdom. Proverbs 11:2

Chapter 68

Sometimes You Just Need to Sit on the Beach for a While

There is so much peace and calmness that comes from sitting and relaxing on the beach or in a meadow or a forest. I love the sounds and abundant people-watching, the waves crashing on the shore, the birds chirping and the sound of laughter, the music and the sound of a softball hitting a glove, the sound of the wind as it makes the umbrellas flap and flags snap, the seagulls calling, and the sun warming my face.

Close your eyes and imagine it for a minute. You can feel it, can't you?

We must all take some time to chill. It might be a beach or somewhere else of your liking, but you must take time to rest your weary body and slow it down for a while.

My grandma always says, "Your health is your wealth." Remember that. Taking time to recharge is of utmost importance, so do it. Never get too busy working that you forget how to live.

By the seventh day God had finished the work he had been doing; so on the seventh day he rested from all his work. Then God blessed the seventh day and made it holy, because on it he rested from all the work of creating that he had done. Genesis 2:2–3

Return to your rest, my soul,
for the LORD has been good to you. Psalm 116:7

Chapter 69

Time, Precious Time

T ime is our most valuable asset, yet the one we most waste. Ask anyone what they would do if they could get a do-over and I bet the majority of people would say something about going back in time to be with someone they loved and lost.

It is the everyday life moments that seem to matter most, the little things a loved one does or says, a routine, joke, or saying. What matters is holding hands, relaxing together, playing together, sharing your life with vulnerability. What matters are long hugs, kind words, and kisses that say, "I love you."

If only I had more blessed time, I would . . .

How do you spend your prized and highly valuable time? Do you waste it?

I think that the most treasured truth I have learned over the years is that there is nothing more central to a balanced life than truly spending time with your family and the ones you love. It is about giving them your full attention and appreciation when with them. I know it sounds difficult. Trust me, I struggle with it too.

Our phones are glued to our sides and there is a constant clamor from the outside world demanding our attention. That stuff isn't important. No one at the end of their life is ever going to say, "I wish I spent more time on my work email. That really would have made a difference."

Time is what is most cherished. The little things are the most important.

So why don't most of us value it now? We waste so much time doing things that don't mean anything, all while the most invaluable asset depletes. You cannot get it back. You cannot buy it. You cannot trade it. Once it is gone, it is gone forever.

Whatever is distracting you from your family or the ones you love, put it down and walk away.

Cherish these moments, the spectacularly irreplaceable points in time that you will never, ever get back. Take them all in. Hold them close to your heart. Guard them and don't let the world distract you from spending your time wisely, filled with things that truly matter.

Be fiercely present and pay attention to those around you. Trust me, there is nothing more important.

There is a time for everything,
and a season for every activity under the heavens. Ecclesiastes 3:1

Be very careful, then, how you live—not as unwise but as wise, making the
most of every opportunity, because the days are evil. Therefore do not be
foolish but understand what the Lord's will is. Ephesians 5:15–17

Precious time with my beautiful mother.

Chapter 70

Four Things to Help Balance Your Life

Let's face it, we live in a world where many of us could work eighty-plus hours a week, and some do! Here are four things I have done in business that have helped me take back my life and my time.

When you read this, especially if you have an A-Type personality like me, they might sound nearly impossible to do. I assure you they are possible. I have done them, and I do them now. Take this advice from someone who has been both places. I wasted way too much time in my life until I started taking these important steps for balancing work and home life.

1. Change your work voicemail to state your hours and stick to them. Set boundaries and expectations. If people know them ahead of time, they will be okay with them.

For example, part of my work voicemail states that if you are calling after work hours or on the weekends, I will return your phone call the next business day, which saves me from having to answer my phone in the evenings or on weekends. Everyone understands.

2. Take your work email off your phone.

This one about gave me a heart attack when I started doing it about a year ago. Now it is one of the best things I have done for sure. It will eliminate the anxiety that comes from being able to preview things work-related when you are not at work.

3. Take notifications off your phone.

This was the other one that nearly caused me to pass out when I did it. After about two days though, it felt great. I check my texts and emails on my terms. I realized that all of those notifications stressed me out and not seeing them pop up every ten seconds has been a tremendous blessing. Trust me on this one.

4. When you are home, be home. Stop working. Go spend time with others.

Most days, I just plug my phone in when I get home, unless I am playing music or chit-chatting with other family and friends. Otherwise, even though my phone is near me, I don't have to pay attention to it.

A funny thing happened when I started doing this, my productivity actually increased. The world didn't end. I took my life back. When I worked, I worked, and when I was done, I was actually done.

For all of you folks who have the opportunity to work from home, this advice is of utmost importance for you also. Having worked from home in the past, I know how blurred the lines between work and home can become. You have to shut it down at a specific time, even when you are already home.

You won't regret it. I promise.

Spend your time on what matters.

"Show me, LORD, my life's end
and the number of my days;
let me know how fleeting my life is.
You have made my days a mere handbreadth;
the span of my years is as nothing before you.

Everyone is but a breath,
even those who seem secure." Psalm 39:4–5

Now listen, you who say, "Today or tomorrow we will go to this or that city, spend a year there, carry on business and make money." Why, you do not even know what will happen tomorrow. What is your life? You are a mist that appears for a little while and then vanishes. Instead, you ought to say, "If it is the Lord's will, we will live and do this or that." As it is, you boast in your arrogant schemes. All such boasting is evil. If anyone, then, knows the good they ought to do and doesn't do it, it is sin for them. James 4:13–17

Chapter 71

Don't Be a Diotrephes

You probably don't know who the heck I'm talking about . . . yet. In the Bible (3 John), there is a self-seeking troublemaker memorialized for being an influential first-class numbskull who abused his authority.

He gossiped, was unhospitable, and brought others down. Then, he wrote off anyone who didn't agree with him. He was a leader because he wanted power, not because he had good intentions or wanted to help people.

So that got me to thinking about why power corrupts some people? Then power-seekers think they can get away with it. Power reveals whether we are a giver or a taker.

Having power actually makes someone *more* responsible for their actions. Many believe that more resources make for less accountability, but the opposite is actually true.

When you are in a position of authority, it is important to hold this opportunity with respect. If you are fortunate enough to be a leader, be one that is looked up to and revered.

Be self-aware and credible. Be humble and authentic. Empower others around you. Be the one who others look up to and want to emulate.

And for goodness' sake don't be a Diotrephes.

I wrote to the church, but Diotrephes, who loves to be first, will not welcome us. So when I come, I will call attention to what he is doing, spreading malicious nonsense about us. Not satisfied with that, he even refuses to welcome other believers. He also stops those who want to do so and puts them out of the church.

Dear friend, do not imitate what is evil but what is good. Anyone who does what is good is from God. Anyone who does what is evil has not seen God. Demetrius is well spoken of by everyone—and even by the truth itself. We also speak well of him, and you know that our testimony is true.
3 John 9–12

Chapter 72

Behave

I f you have ever traveled for work, you know what mean here. You can find out quickly what other people are *really* like.

I used to travel a lot with my old employer. Team trips and manager's meetings were peppered throughout the year. Spouses were not invited, and most people welcomed that. I was single at the time, but it used to make me so sad to see my colleagues' true colors. They weren't pretty. They were one person at home and then when they were "set free" in the wild, they became someone else and behaved quite badly. They must have thought that no one was looking, but the truth is, we all were.

I remember one particular evening after a work dinner in Dallas that ran late, one of the higher ups in Dallas disappeared for a while and then came back. By then, a bunch of people had gathered for a nightcap at the bar. I was one of them.

He came back down and very boastingly told everyone he had pretended to be in bed (he had got in bed and pulled up the covers) and FaceTimed his wife to tell her goodnight and that he was going to sleep. He then left his phone in the room and came down to the bar to play. There were two sets of reactions that night. Some, like me, were mortified. I felt so sorry for his wife and family and lost my respect for him. Others were like, "Wow, that is a great idea." They laughed like it was something to be celebrated. I went to bed.

What a horrible example. That begs the question: Who are you when you spouse is not around? Your answer says a lot about your character.

As Christians, we are to be good examples. We have to set our bars high when it comes to our conduct.

When you travel, don't stay out late and drink all night. Don't lie to your spouse about your plans. Resist temptation by not putting yourself into situations where your beliefs and vows can be compromised. If you are a leader in the company, act like one. Set a good example for your team. Put yourself in the shoes of your spouse and ask yourself, *Would my spouse approve of this behavior?*" You already know the answer.

Look, I know what it is like out there. I know that there are obligatory dinners which sometimes require a drink afterwards. No one says you have to have three drinks. Have one and then go to bed. Don't even put yourself out there to do anything else. It is safer, and that way you will never regret any of your actions. You will stay true to yourself, your marriage, and your faith.

Behave.

"Whoever would love life
and see good days
must keep their tongue from evil
and their lips from deceitful speech.
They must turn from evil and do good;
they must seek peace and pursue it.
For the eyes of the Lord are on the righteous
and his ears are attentive to their prayer,
but the face of the Lord is against those who do evil." 1 Peter 3:10–12

"Therefore what God has joined together, let no one separate." Mark 10:9

Chapter 73

Trust That Gut of Yours

I have learned that when there are roadblocks in every direction, whatever I'm doing is not something I should do. I have learned this lesson over and over, and now I've learned it once again.

Whenever I have forced something to happen in my life (like where I will work or a house I want to buy—something I want or *think* I want or believe is a good idea—but God isn't behind it, He is always right.

He sends me roadblock after roadblock and a feeling I get in the pit of my stomach. Those are my red flags, and they always siren loudly. He does it every single time, yet sometimes I still choose not to listen.

When I don't, it usually ends in disaster.

Intuition is a powerful thing. I always tell people that it is how God talks to me and gives me insight. Still, sometimes I don't listen because I feel like I know better or something.

Even if the data, numbers, and promises look great on paper, if you still get a feeling in the pit of your stomach that there is something wrong, it should not be ignored.

If, at every turn, there is a complication popping up, listen to your gut. Stop forcing the issue. It is time to move on.

Whether it be alarm bells ringing or a twinge of hesitation, you should listen to it. Give things a second thought and get down to the bottom of what is causing the feeling. I'll bet you it is God trying to tell you to walk or run away. Listen to Him.

I urge you, brothers and sisters, to watch out for those who cause divisions and put obstacles in your way that are contrary to the teaching you have learned. Keep away from them. Romans 16:17

Do not be anxious about anything, but in every situation, by prayer and petition, with thanksgiving, present your requests to God. Philippians 4:6

Chapter 74

When You Finally Figure Out What You Are Supposed to Do

love stories about people who thrive because they are finally doing what they God meant for them to do. Oh, how they thrive.

It is as if a switch flips and suddenly their engine hums like a finely tuned motor. Perfection.

The power that comes from this is magnificent, isn't it? Wow, if we could all do that, imagine the world we would live in!

A humming of angels singing, "Hallelujah" would fill the earth. Everyone would be using the gifts that God blessed them with for the purposes He designed us to fulfill. That would be a beautiful thing.

There are some of us who have figured out our gifts and purpose, but we are too afraid to let go of the material world we live in to make things happen as they should. It is scary, I know. I have been there.

One day, I hope we all realize it before it is too late. When we do, we are going to want to kick ourselves (as I have) because we will realize we could have been doing it all along. You will get it. Everything will work out so much better than your mind can fathom right now, but when you actually start doing it, you will be wildly successful.

God shows us glimpses of our future. He showed me that my words (His words too) will inspire many. To get here though, I had to give up everything—or so I thought. Turns out that I gained so much more when I finally surrendered to His will.

My wish for you is that you use the gifts God blessed you with. Come to Him. Run to Him. He will give you the strength to get through the day, and He will give you the courage to live the life He intended for you—one day at a time, every day, until you spend eternity with Him.

Use your gifts wisely. Don't waste your precious life being scared to do what God intended you to do.

We have different gifts, according to the grace given to each of us. If your gift is prophesying, then prophesy in accordance with your faith; if it is serving, then serve; if it is teaching, then teach; if it is to encourage, then give encouragement; if it is giving, then give generously; if it is to lead, do it diligently; if it is to show mercy, do it cheerfully. Romans 12:6–8

One Size Does Not Fit All

While there is no one size fits all formula for monetary success in the workplace, know that if you keep God in the center of all you do, you will be successful in the things that matter. Each of our journeys will be different, but the struggles we have are very much the same.

Are there things that you can do to make a difference in how you approach your work?

Epilogue

My dear friend, I am so happy to have been able to spend this time with you. Thank you for sharing your wisdom, your struggles, and your testimony with me. I hope that I, in some way, helped you with my stories.

Remember that you are *never* alone. God is with you, always.

Until next time—

Jen

About the Author

Hello friends! It has been a joy to connect with you all. My life's journey has taken me through peaks and valleys, each one offering valuable lessons that I am privileged to share with others. One of my passions, as you have read, that fuels my spirit, is hiking. There's something magical that unfolds with each step, just as the chapters of our lives unravel. In those peaceful moments, I find clarity and strength that I bring to my writing.

Through my books, my goal is to uplift, encourage and remind all who read them that life's challenges are merely steppingstones to a higher purpose. I aim to kindle hope and ignite faith in the hearts of every reader.

Thank you for joining me on this incredible journey. To find out more about what I do, visit BrilliantlyBold.com.

www.ingramcontent.com/pod-product-compliance
Lightning Source LLC
Chambersburg PA
CBHW022127080426
42734CB00006B/264